Intimate Leadership

Build Powerful, Profitable,
Consumer-Products Brands, and Companies.

Jayaram Rajaram

INDIA • SINGAPORE • MALAYSIA

ISBN 979-8-89133-733-6

Disclaimer

All information shared in this book is purely for educational purposes and from the Author's own experiences and study. You explicitly indemnify the Author of any losses you may incur by adopting any of the strategies written about. The Author has not taken any monetary compensation from any of the organizations he has written about. The Author may have investments in shares in some of the public companies he has written about. His investments have no relation to the matter published in this book and are not an endorsement by the Author to invest in the said companies. With respect to unlisted companies also, no monetary compensation has been received to feature the said companies in this book. Wherever there is any independent commercial agreement with any company, the same has been explicitly disclosed by the author for purposes transparency.

Contents

Intimate Leadership

Build Powerful, Profitable, Consumer-Products Brands and Companies.

Jayaram Rajaram

"Leadership is a journey.
The journey is the reward".

– Shiv Shivakumar

Ex Chairman and CEO PepsiCo India, Ex Group Executive President – Corporate Strategy & Business Development Aditya Birla Group and Operating Partner Advent International

"A simple yet deep sharing of business and leadership insights by Jayaram with his firsthand experience in running Bril. He peppers the book with first hand details of running a business and also multiple examples of his reading and analysis over the years. Valuable for everyone wanting to learn how to build and run businesses."

– Anil Viswanathan

VP and Managing Director, Mondelez Vietnam

"A very simple well-articulated first principles perspective not just to business, branding, marketing, positioning, and sales but also covers the importance of value systems and of Human Resource Capital. Besides being an enjoyable read, the book is more than a business journey across generations offering not only an engaging narrative but also valuable insights into navigating the trials of change and turbulences of the business world."

– Prem Kumar

Founder & CEO SnapBizz CloudTech Pvt. Ltd.
Serial Entrepreneur, Ex President SE Asia Reckitt Benckiser,
Head Sales and Marketing LAKME LEVER

Acknowledgements

I thank from the bottom of my heart, my parents, my wife, and my children for giving me my safe place called home and always encouraging me to pursue my passions. Writing this book has been a deeply personal yet rewarding journey as I was able to fondly relive the years gone by in my entrepreneurial journey. The years go by fast! I thank God every day for making me be born into a family that is not only so loving, but so rooted in Indian cultural traditions and middle-class values. I sincerely thank my grandfather, father, my spiritual Gurus, and God for giving me the opportunity to manage a brand that is so close to the hearts of hundreds of millions of consumers across generations. I fondly remember and thank Late Dr. Bala V Balachandran (Uncle Bala), my guru of the material world, for being my mentor, guide, and friend. I thank my entire team at Bril for always being by my side in my good days and bad and building something great in India, for India! I thank leaders of all the companies I have admired, researched, and written about, for the phenomenal learnings and leadership insights they have given people like me and other entrepreneurs to learn from.

I am truly grateful to Mr. Vijay Parthasarathy Global CEO, #1Bestselling Author/Mind Coach/Brand Specialist/ Motivational Speaker, for being a mentor who speaks the unfiltered truth to help me, by sharing his vast experience in global leadership and brand-building. I am truly humbled by his words of appreciation for my book, in the Foreword that he very kindly wrote after reading the entire book in one day!

I thank Mr. Shiv Shivakumar Ex Chairman and CEO PepsiCo India, Ex Group Executive President – Corporate Strategy & Business Development Aditya Birla Group and Operating Partner Advent International who taught me and inspired me when I was in BSchool, for reading, appreciating the book and kindly writing a few insightful words about 'The Many Facets of Leadership'. I thank my friends, mentors and family who are outstanding leaders who have taken the time to read, give feedback and appreciate the book.

I wanted to put the picture of my late Grandfather Dr. N. Jayaraman here, so nobody forgets his contribution to Indian entrepreneurship and service to Indian consumers:

Foreword

You are wandering through a forest and it is one thing to have a carefully scripted guide to take you across. But it is a completely different ball game when someone who has crossed that jungle just a few weeks earlier accompanies you. That is exactly the feeling that I got when Jayaram put forth this task of penning this foreword. You walk away at the end feeling awed by the lucidity and authenticity with which each and every case study is presented. A narrative written mainly in first person provides you with this freshness as he takes you through the exploration of his family business of Bril, the multiple challenges, the dreams that never took off, and then exhilaration at the success as they found the pot of gold at the end of the rainbow. Not once but multiple times.

But clearly, it is evident what constitutes leadership in general and what Jayaram anoints it with the word 'intimate'

Be it Mukesh Ambani or the Bhagavad Gita, the singular message that paves the way for the most successful leaders is Courage. Courage – the ability to take that leap of faith based on gut instinct though everyone around you is scaring you to avoid. The ability to know that in risking and burning the boat is where the freedom and glory lie. Time and again in Jayaram's treatise this hits home. Be it taking on new products the world had shunned, innovating with payment methods introduced in the distribution system that could mean a huge dip in revenues, or making the life-changing decision to get out of Amazon – that is courage and Jayaram has shown in no uncertain terms how in each instance they were either hugely successful or learnt something that was invaluable.

Jayaram also displays his vulnerability in a manner that touches one's heart as he takes you on the journey of failures of either hiring the wrong CEO or onboarding brand extensions that went bust or – most powerfully – taking you through his mental journey post-COVID. This requires courage too. And that's what he terms 'intimate leadership' – clearly going to places where no one has been and knowing very well that failure is an orphan that not many would want to embrace.

The book also seamlessly navigates you through intricate financial models of revenue and profit graphs and valuation models and matrices with price elasticity thrown in with the ease of an expert ice skater walking on cemented roads.

Importantly, Jayaram touches extensively on my favourite subject, the MIND. The power of this amazing and mighty instrument with which we come into this world but are not provided with the instruction manual and most go through a trial-and-error methodology to unearth the same. Once again 'Intimate leadership'.

He highlights the importance of meditation and mindfulness and how they can truly be the forerunners of excellence in this fast-paced world of 'uncertainty and insecurity-driven chaos.'

One of the basics of every single legendary leader is their die-hard adherence to values, the foundation sans which every vision and mission statement would be a mere placard behind the CEO's office desk.

I loved the way he coins this phrase of 'Social norms outweighing market norms' and that is very much a part of every activity by which his family business has led its 60-plus-year journey.

Finally, the essence of the Bhagavad Gita comes into play as 'Nishkama Karma' the ability to focus on your task without the expectation of results, finds its roots on the organization's mantle.

This truly is a book packed with incredible content that will make the reader thirsting for more even as she goes through multiple readings.

I would like to congratulate Jayaram on this awesome effort and am sure every reader will find his own 'Wow!' moment as he traverses this journey.

– Vijay Parthasarathy

Global CEO, #1Bestselling Author/Mind Coach/
Brand Specialist/Motivational Speaker
Bestselling Book: ***The Golden Ladder: Rise To Be Unstoppable***

The Many Facets of Leadership

Shiv Shivakumar's thoughts on Leadership

Leadership is an ever-discussed topic and there are many theories of how leaders should function and what leadership means. I have read many books on leadership, and I am happy to see Jayaram pen his thoughts on this important topic.

Leadership is about the mind, your ability to make people think differently. For you to achieve any degree of success in this aspect, you must have credibility.

Credibility in leadership is about several things.

It's about performance, it's about fairness, it's about contribution beyond the job, it's about inspiring people.

You can only have credibility if you have done something significant in the roles you have performed and if you have left a legacy in the roles you have done. Performance is about impact in the job, it's about going well beyond the job description. A leadership role has no definition, each leader brings his or her take to the job. Leaders tend to redefine the job to suit their personality and their ability to push a clear mandate for change.

You will have credibility if you have been fair in your dealings with the ecosystem and your evaluation of contribution in the team and organization. Many leaders tend to read the data and the situation with rose tinted glasses. The ability to read the data in the same manner irrespective of who presents the data is important for leaders. Leaders at one level need to perform in areas they are good at and at another level, take the analogy of cricket, if the captain is a batsman, he needs to perform, that automatically gets him respect and leverage when he leads the side. If a captain doesn't get runs or wickets, then his/her credibility is dented.

Inspiring people is about connecting the dots and communicating that insightfully. A leader's ability to be insightful and hence the ability to paint a picture of the future is energizing. Remember John F Kennedy's words "we will put a man on the moon and bring him back safely before the end of this decade" That sentence inspired NASA, America, and the whole scientific community in America.

Inspiring requires high levels of communication skills. Leaders need to practice their speeches and edit their notes many times before delivering it. It could end up as a non – stop stream of messaging but that's the expectation from the job.

Communication must be done in an authentic manner. Some American leaders like Steve Ballmer tend to scream, jump around on stage etc. That's unlikely to work in Asia where they expect leaders to be understated but effective. Choosing a style of communication is important for a leader. My input – don't try to be someone you are not.

When leaders discuss communication, everyone wants to communicate like Steve Jobs and Obama. That takes a lot of effort and sacrifice. Good leaders tend to focus on communicating a max of three messages in a speech or a note and back up the rest of the speech and note to back the three points.

Being a leader is not easy in a disruptive and innovative world. Leaders must take solace that the journey is the reward and hence worth it.

– Shiv Shivakumar

Ex Chairman and CEO PepsiCo India, Ex Group Executive President – Corporate Strategy & Business Development Aditya Birla Group and Operating Partner Advent International.

More Praise for the Book:

"Intimate Leadership," is a captivating exploration of timeless strategies to create enduring and thriving consumer-products brands. In this extraordinary odyssey, Jayaram shares invaluable insights and anecdotes from his 21 years of building the legacy of Bril.

Originally an iconic fountain pen ink brand that transcended generations, Bril now spans multiple categories, touching the lives of over 480 million consumers in its illustrious 60-year voyage. Jayaram's first-hand account delves into his strongly held leadership values weaving it seamlessly with the doggedness of long-term Brand Building that keeps Bril eternally relevant in our rapidly evolving world.

This book isn't just a memoir; it's a treasure trove of wisdom. As Jayaram reveals the secrets that breathe life into legendary brands and fuel the rise of nimble startups, you'll embark on a journey that bridges the gap between heritage and innovation. "Intimate Leadership" is a testament to the power of emotional connections, teaching you how to craft consumer-products brands that stand the test of time, forever etching their mark in the hearts and minds of consumers.

Immerse yourself in this book, to learn how to build a great, profitable, and enduring consumer products company. This isn't theory that needs to be proven in the market, but an account of actual in-market action and real consumer responses.

– Sharavana Raghavan

Brand Expert, Founder Vitral Brand Expertise
www.vitral.in

While there are tons of literature available that talks about leadership - most of what I have read are either abstract or too conceptual. Leading a business is an everyday learning - very personal and contextual. So, it's a challenging task to come up with a very practical working guide for practising entrepreneurs.

But surprisingly Jayaram has brilliantly crystallized the wisdom from leading a business successfully for 20+ years and articulated it so well. This book has come up at the right time when the New Bharat is thriving with a new-age entrepreneurial spirit. Reading this book can be the best investment of time for someone running a business.

– Gangadharan A

Partner, LFC Consulting Practice LLP; Director,
LFC Digital Solutions Pvt Ltd
www.leversforchange.in | www.connectfacts.com

Written in a simple narrative style, Jayaram's book contains numerous stories and anecdotes which prove that with strong core values, ethics, and principles, an organisation can scale and run an enduring business. All leaders and entrepreneurs, regardless of the size of their organisation, will find some useful takeaways.

– Ganapathy Sankarabaaham

Chief Executive, Vajra Global Consulting Services
www.vajraglobal.com

Intimate Leadership

My name is Jayaram Rajaram, and I am the Managing Partner of a company (Industrial Research Corporation) that became famous for its fountain pen inks – Bril Inks. My grandfather was a scientist who worked and did his post-doctoral at Indian Institute of Science before he started this company that makes Bril Inks, stationery products and other consumer products today. When he started the company, it was a one product company, but a very important one that has set the tone for the decades to come. He formulated fountain pen inks and started selling the ink he made on his bicycle after quitting his research job as a post-doctoral scientist at The Indian Institute of Science Bangalore.

My father is the second-generation leader who has nurtured and grown this brand over the years and continues to guide me and the team today. I consider myself very fortunate to be able to nurture this brand with my father's help, as a third-generation entrepreneur, ably assisted by my phenomenal intimate team.

Many of my friends ask me why we have stayed a relatively small, closely held family business? They ask, 'Why haven't you raised VC/PE money?', 'Why no IPO?' These are recurrent questions, and I would be lying if I said I have never thought of fund raising and faster growth post my MBA.

But in entrepreneurship, sometimes a little bit of laziness is sometimes good because one can sleep better without having to answer questions that taking money brings along with it. There is no free lunch and raising capital brings with it the stress and obligation of having to answer investors and sometimes do things that we wouldn't do otherwise, for the sake of growth and many times, growth at the cost of value-creation! Do I have anything against the VC ecosystem or new-age startups? No way! My book is my perspective and trust me that there is never one way to do business.

This book is primarily about leadership from my own experience of over 21 years of managing Bril, which is an Indian consumer-products brand (www.brilindia.com) that has till date conservatively touched more than 480 million consumers. Beyond my perspective, I will also be discussing examples of some legendary brands to drive home points and perspectives on how to build profitable consumer-products brands, specifically for India. However, the book can be used by entrepreneurs world over, as most parts of the book apply to all markets. My goal is to give entrepreneurs timeless tools and strategies to build and grow a profitable consumer-products brand and organization, in this ever-changing world of B2C (Business to Consumer), B2B2C (Business to Business to Consumer) and D2C (Direct to Consumer) buzzwords.

Most importantly, I will not be sharing my company's turnover or profits because we are still a closely held family business (a benefit of not raising external capital 😉! Also asking us for our turnover and profits is like me asking you for your salary! 😉)! Jokes apart and more importantly it is not needed for the subject covered by this book. The important thing is that we have been in business for 60 years and by God's grace have been profitable for 57 years of the 60 years. Of the three unprofitable years two years were due to Covid where we only managed to do 30% or our normal turnover due to schools being closed. I owe a lot to this business, my grandfather and father, as this business has paid for my good education, given me a good life, given 1000s of people employment directly and indirectly and now that I am managing the business, a worthy purpose. So, the most important thing that you would take away from this book are leadership insights, systems and strategies that could help you build a REAL profitable consumer-products business, with people at its core, that can stand the test of time.

The point is to write about my experience from the heart while also sharing timeless principles that would help leaders build their own profitable consumer-products brands and companies.

* * * * *

Your Leadership Team's Ethics Makes or Breaks a Business – It's Not Always Smooth Sailing

My Grandfather started Bril in 1964 and made his nephews (his sister's sons) my father's cousins Mr. Sethuraman and Mr. Viswanathan his partners in the partnership firm. My father's cousins were gems and some of the most ethical partners and this was of great strength to my grandfather and subsequently my father. My grandfather had seen many ups and downs in his life and business prior to starting Bril, with breaches of trust and more, but it was his elder brother, my Grand Uncle Late Mr. N. Raghunathan Iyer, who stood by him like a pillar of strength as the oldest among the brothers, though he was not at all a part of the company. In fact, Mr. Raghunathan Iyer was in employment as The Associate Editor of The Hindu Newspaper. In 1971, my grandfather passed away of a massive cardiac arrest following the failure of his big pet project, a furnace to smelt minerals and make thermo-phosphates. This project had left the family in huge debts and my father was still studying for his PhD in Northwestern University, Chicago, USA. Upon my other Grand Uncle (My grandfather's youngest brother) Mr. Balasundaram's insistence, my father returned to the US after completing my grandfather's last rites, to complete his PhD in inorganic chemistry. While my father was away, my father's cousins (Mr. Sethuraman and Mr. Viswanathan) and their father Mr. Rajagopal Iyer along with my Grand Uncle Mr. Balasundaram (A visionary industrialist based in Faridabad associated with the Birla group in his day), managed Bril. While Bril was doing well, the profits were meagre, despite good volume sales. It was upon Mr. Balasundaram's visionary and intuitive guidance that the price of Bril Ink was doubled (exact MRP at the time is not clear) and that in addition to sale of various properties helped the family settle all the debts. My father, me and my family owe an immense debt of gratitude to Mr. N.Raghunathan, Mr. Balasundaram, Mr. Sethuraman and Mr. Viswanathan for helping us when things were looking very bleak for the business and family. Mr. Raghunathan and Mr. Balasundaram did all this with zero stake or commercial gain from the business. They did it for the love of their brother and their brother's children. In the toughest of times, it was my Grand Uncles and my father's cousins who cared for and nurtured the business, till my father and uncle could take charge. Can you imagine such acts of selflessness in today's purely commercial world? Do you think there was any chance of Bril surviving with the untimely passing of my grandfather (the founder) and the family reeling in debt due to the failure of another business venture, without the support of steadfast ethical leadership by my grandfather's elder and younger brothers? The importance of good mentors and an ethical leadership team cannot be more highly emphasized.

Subsequently my father and Uncle joined the partnership and started managing the business along with their cousins, under the guidance of my Grand Uncle. My uncle, Mr. Kasinathan (my father's own brother) who eventually started his own electronics company, has always been there physically, as a partner and emotionally for my father. I am always thankful to my uncle who till date stands by my father and me, no matter what. Subsequently, one of my father's cousins passed away prematurely and the other cousin retired at the age of 60 after being there for my father and being a karma yogi. Why did I narrate this story? Firstly, to give you the history of how Bril was started, and more importantly to tell you that ethics is paramount. The lack of ethics amongst family members or unrelated cofounders can seriously jeopardize the future of any business. Human relationships are complicated even without commercial relationships, so imagine family members being business partners also! So, after all these trials and tribulations, if Bril as a brand has survived for nearly 60 years, it is only thanks to the Grace of the Almighty and all the people he has sent our way to contribute to its sustenance and growth – It's not always smooth sailing! So, be extremely careful while selecting your core leadership team if you are yet to start off. Core values and ethics trumps everything else in running and scaling an enduring business.

This book is about Bril, yet it is not about Bril – it is much more than that. It is about how we can all build enduring, profitable consumer products brands and organizations. In the coming chapters I will move seamlessly between my experiences managing Bril and lessons from legendary and up-coming consumer products brands. I have written this book as much for myself and my family as I have for you, the reader.

* * * * *

The Product isn't Everything

Till a few decades ago, product quality was a differentiator. Today, in the hyper-competitive market landscape, a high-quality product is not only non-negotiable but is just the starting point. Moreover, one no longer needs to manufacture products in their own factories anymore. If you have an idea, rest assured there would be someone who has a factory that could make it into a product for you. This wasn't the case 20-30 years ago, as manufacturing your own product in your own factory was wrongly seen as a major differentiator and cost advantage. This differentiator was and is however short-lived, because another more state-of-the-art factory can make a better, faster, cheaper product and you would be out of business. At Bril, we manufacture 30% of our products in our own factory, while the rest is outsourced to factories all over India (We only source 2% of our products from China and Korea). We are a proud Indian brand providing employment to 1000s of families directly and indirectly. Did you know that NIKE doesn't own any factory? NIKE products are actually manufactured across 41 countries, with the help of 533 factories and 1.1million workers. Nike's factories are outsourced, meaning that they don't own the actual facility and they 'contract' the factories to produce for them based on strict SOPs, quality checks and protocols. While Apple designs and sells the iPhone and other Apple products, it doesn't manufacture its components. Instead, Apple uses manufacturers from around the world to deliver individual parts. So, what differentiates the top brands like Apple, Nike, TATA, Starbucks, Google, Microsoft, P&Gs brands, Unilever's brands etc? For every NIKE there are thousands of other shoe brands, but there is something in that Swoosh that sets Nike apart. Why do people queue up to buy that iPhone when there are thousands of other phones at lower prices and very often with better features? As entrepreneurs, we have to think hard about how we can create these moats and learn from the stalwarts. So, brand-building is an art and a science, and we need to master that. So how do we start?

Let's start by defining a brand. **I define a brand as a name/word/image/logo given to a core functional product that solves a consumer/customer problem/need reliably and repeatedly. A powerful brand is one that forms an emotional chord between the brand and the consumer, through shared experiences, and becomes a part of the collective consumer consciousness with the passage of time.**

Most brands are, as I call them Superficial Brands. I define Superficial Brands as any brand that has a name/logo but lacks depth because it hasn't yet built a deep emotional connect/bond through shared experiences with its consumers. Consumers are still its fair-weather friends and not its BFFs (Best Friends Forever).

So, the operative word in the above paragraphs and what differentiates a powerful super brand from a superficial brand is the word 'emotional'. All powerful brands tug at our emotional chords. If brands remain in the functional realm, they are open to disruption by new entrants or existing competitors who one-up them on functionality and/or benefits.

As a leader, the most important thing you need to do is to ask yourself what emotional business are you in? Forget your product or service, forget features and benefits. What are the emotional chords that you would tug at when a customer interacts with your brand?

Think hard and understand which emotion your brand stands for. Emotions can broadly be classified into LOVE, NOSTALGIA, JOY/FUN, FEAR (Negative Emotion), PRIDE (Status), FREEDOM, TRUST. However, the underlying primary positive emotion that plays out is love for oneself, love for others, love for possessions/money etc. I say this because, for human-beings, emotions will always trump logic whether we accept it or not. This is something I have always spoken about, understood and try my best to use in my own business. Having said this, building a brand that subconsciously tugs at the same emotional chords of consumers, over decades requires consistence, persistence, and a long-term mindset. While on this topic, I really enjoyed reading The Golden Ladder Rise To Be Unstoppable by Vijay Parthasarathy that analyses the emotions involved with respect to brand-building very well.

* * * * *

So, How Do You Build a Powerful Brand?

All the world's best brands have been built by leveraging these core emotions and have been etched into our subconscious minds. If you think about it, what Sylvester Dacunha has done over the years with the Amul girl and situational marketing is epic beyond words. There won't be too many Indians who won't remember the tag line 'Utterly Butterly Delicious'. Do you think Amul cared for immediate sales, or cares for immediate measurable sales when they advertise situationally? No way! Amul's story is a classic example of how a brand is built in the consumer's mind day after day, year after year, decade after decade. So, what emotional chord does Amul cater to? Their ads revolve typically around humour, so FUN is a major emotion they cater to along with the LOVE and craving for awesome food that's shared with loved ones!

In today's world of digital marketing, most entrepreneurs focus too much on performance marketing and measurability of campaigns like Conversion rates, Click Through Rates (CTR), Cost Per Click (CPC), Cost Per Mille (CPM), ROAS (Return on Advertising Spend) etc. Am I saying measurement is bad? Not at all. I understand that startups have to be frugal, and it is absolutely essential and important to be profitable as soon as possible and not burn cash for too long. But sadly, the opposite is happening

– despite all measurements, startups are haemorrhaging cash and bleeding like crazy for years, running for the next infusion of funds from investors, who too are pushing for growth at any cost. Brand building, however, is a long-term game, and companies should understand the importance of performance marketing and brand marketing going hand-in-hand to build long-term brand equity. For example, at Bril we have been printing 50000-1 lakh Calendars every year for nearly 50 years now. Who uses calendars these days right? You would be surprised to note that our calendars are loved and looked forward to by several households in southern India. Shopkeeper's pay to have their shop names printed on the Bril Calendar and distribute it to their networks. Our calendar is loved for its BIG display of dates and easy-to-read-from-a-distance design. Imagine your brand being visible day after day for the whole year in your customer's home or workplace. We have images of our entire range of products, category-wise printed on different months of the year on the calendar. We also used to print notebook labels with our branding for decades and are restarting it this year after a short hiatus. We are there with millions of students, every day of their academic year on the covers of their notebooks. This is consumer intimacy. These Below the Line (BTL) Promotion Strategies sound very basic in today's complex digital world, but believe me it's consistency that builds brands. Several super brands like Ramraj vests have been built through wall paintings across tier 2, tier 3 towns. You can't skip a wall painting or a hoarding. When it was in vogue, we distributed branded stepney covers and my father's brainchild had thousands of scooter owners protecting their spare tyre and becoming moving ads for Bril. Further, rural marketing is as simple as it is complex, because building a product and campaigns for rural India cannot be a cut-paste exercise from the urban playbook.

For Brilrider, a balance bike for 1-5-year-olds (India-Patented Design), a predominantly urban-centric brand, we have continuous rotation of Facebook, YouTube and Instagram ads supplemented by Television Advertising during holidays on channels like NickJr (Where parents of toddlers watch with their kids). We use videos submitted by the parents themselves (user generated content). We got several good videos by conducting regular online video contests, where parents would get amazing Brilrider Flight AF prizes for sharing videos of their little ones riding the Brilrider. We measure our overall ad spends on the product and see if it makes sense after 1 year of launching a product. After that we allocate a percentage of sales to ensure ad spends do not burn cash. We realized quickly that performance marketing levels off after a while and beyond the first few months doesn't yield proportionate increase in sales with increase in ad spends, and costs have to go up disproportionately to get the same results (That's how the algorithms work, to help the digital platforms make more money). Standing out from the clutter on television, radio, print and social media with so many channels and so many brands screaming is becoming a marketer's nightmare. We know that we cannot outshout the big brands, so we get innovative with the budgets we have and go super-targeted. Most brands advertising on television today don't get their message across as viewers change channels the minute ads come. On YouTube, the Skip option shouts 'DEATH' for any brand and bleeds money if you are not careful. Though more expensive, it is better to allocate 50% of your YouTube budget to non-skippable ad campaigns options in YouTube where your ads play before, during or after a video and cannot be skipped by the viewer. On channels like Facebook and Instagram, the thumb scrolls away from ads literally in less than a second due to ad fatigue. So, this is where we keep the ads on and push for consistency over immediate results, without increasing budgets disproportionately for immediate results. The brand gets built slowly, but surely, if you have a product that consumers need or aspire for. Pulsing over a period of time across multiple mediums, channels and avenues far outweighs a sprint.

For Inks and fountain pens, we have had handwriting contests for years and the last time we conducted one we gave away cash scholarships worth Rs. 7.5 lakhs. The participation for these contests is absolutely amazing. The only condition we have is that children must use fountain pen ink and a fountain pen to participate. We don't insist on them using Bril fountain pens or Bril Ink. Our objective is to encourage traditional fountain pen usage as we know it helps children with stability-flow balance and helps the environment. I personally write to school Principals encouraging them to get their school children to participate in the contest. It is heartwarming to receive lakhs of entries posted by the schools to our Head Office. This way we know that the schools have conducted the handwriting contest in their premises and hence the children's entries are valid. The last time we conducted a contest was in 2019, just before Covid, and we hope to continue this every few years. My grandfather started it, and my father continued this idea of conducting handwriting contests in schools, when schools used to permit our teams to go in-person and conduct the competition. So again, did this increase sales in the short-term? Maybe. But the consistency of keeping at something that works is what has helped Bril Inks still survive, in addition to of course the grace of the Almighty. It's because of this that millions of parents fondly and nostalgically (emotion) remember Bril Ink when they think of their school days. Will they recommend the Bril brand to their children? We sure hope so, but we continue doing whatever we can do to stay as close to our consumers as possible and help them Make Living Fun! I don't have a big following on LinkedIn, and my posts normally get 15-100 reactions and reach around 1000-20000 people at max. However, a simple post about Bril ink got 5321 impressions, 1270 comments, 48 reposts and 424529 impressions (See post screenshots below).

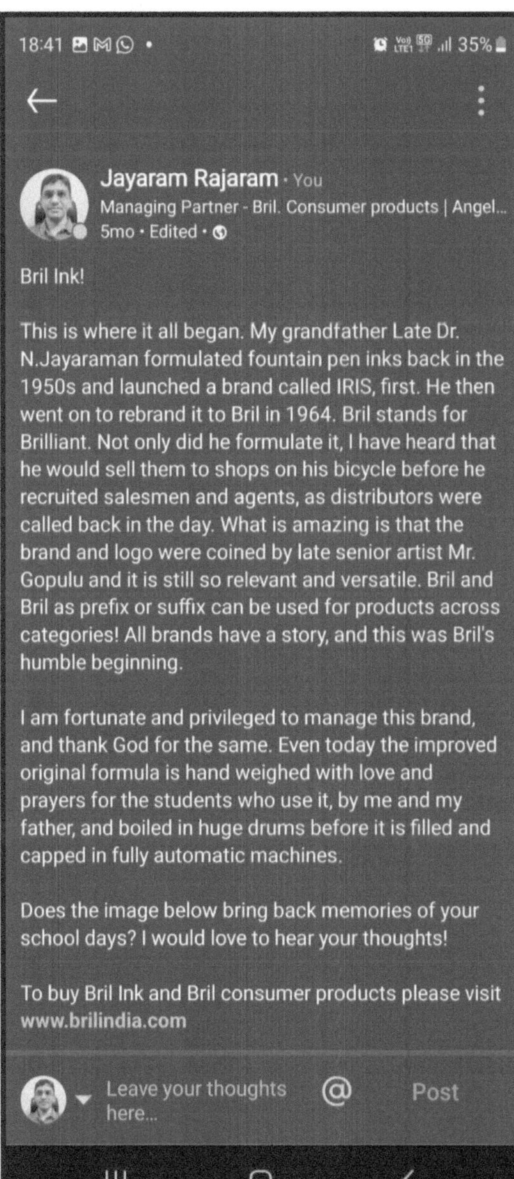
18:41
Jayaram Rajaram · You
Managing Partner - Bril. Consumer products | Angel...
5mo · Edited ·
Bril Ink!
This is where it all began. My grandfather Late Dr. N.Jayaraman formulated fountain pen inks back in the 1950s and launched a brand called IRIS, first. He then went on to rebrand it to Bril in 1964. Bril stands for Brilliant. Not only did he formulate it, I have heard that he would sell them to shops on his bicycle before he recruited salesmen and agents, as distributors were called back in the day. What is amazing is that the brand and logo were coined by late senior artist Mr. Gopulu and it is still so relevant and versatile. Bril and Bril as prefix or suffix can be used for products across categories! All brands have a story, and this was Bril's humble beginning.
I am fortunate and privileged to manage this brand, and thank God for the same. Even today the improved original formula is hand weighed with love and prayers for the students who use it, by me and my father, and boiled in huge drums before it is filled and capped in fully automatic machines.
Does the image below bring back memories of your school days? I would love to hear your thoughts!
To buy Bril Ink and Bril consumer products please visit www.brilindia.com
Leave your thoughts here...
@
Post

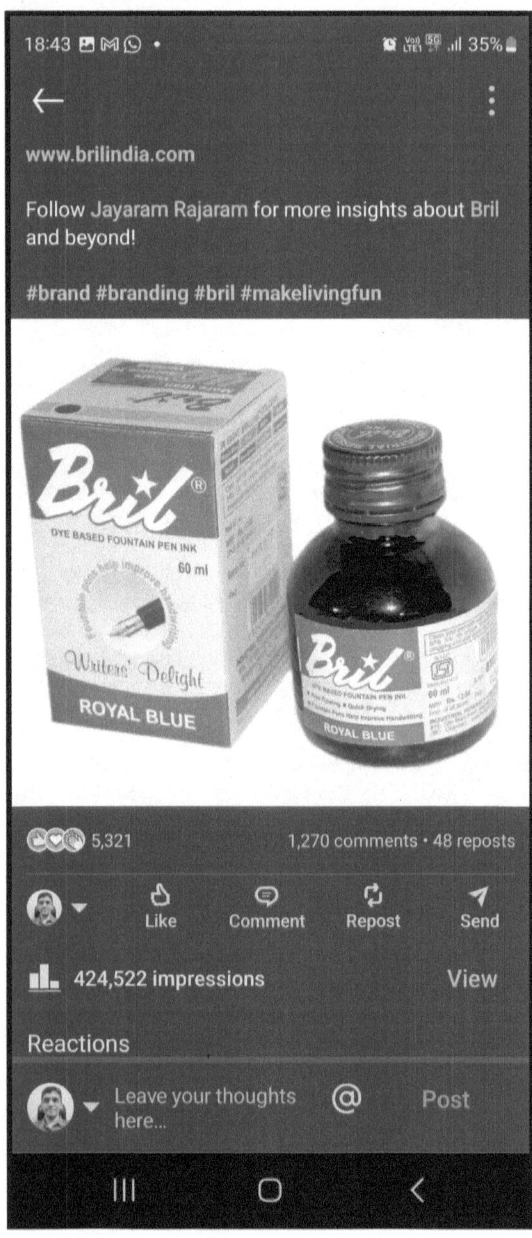

18:43
35%
www.brilindia.com
Follow Jayaram Rajaram for more insights about Bril and beyond!
#brand #branding #bril #makelivingfun
Bril®
DYE BASED FOUNTAIN PEN INK
60 ml
Fountain pens help improve handwriting
Writers' Delight
ROYAL BLUE
Bril®
ROYAL BLUE
5,321
1,270 comments • 48 reposts
Like
Comment
Repost
Send
424,522 impressions
View
Reactions
Leave your thoughts here...
@
Post

Yes, the above post organically reached almost half a million people. Why? Did I do anything great? No. It's unadulterated nostalgia about their school days and shared experiences with their friends and Bril Ink that made so many people take note, react, and share their experiences. It's the sheer joy of great memories of those carefree days when they splashed ink on each other after exams, elated that the exams are over and holidays are about to begin, yet a little sad that they won't see their friends for two months. Why do so many consumers have such a strong connection with Bril Ink? It is because 1000s of people who came before me have kept this brand alive and relevant to consumers. With all this said, we are still work in progress and have made several mistakes along the way but somehow managed to survive because of God's grace, which I will never discount. All brands are work in progress and must keep doing things that make them emotionally and functionally relevant to ever-changing consumer behaviours and market landscapes and dynamics. As you read on, there will be many more examples, leadership and brand stories to make you understand what intimate leadership means and how you should go about it within your organization and in relation to your customers, consumers, and all stakeholders.

Me handing over a scholarship cheque for Rs. 5 Lakhs to a winner of the Handwriting Competition in 2019

* * * * *

Leverage Influencer Marketing and Content Creators

Love them or hate them, today no marketing department can ignore influencers and content creators. It is amazing how the pandemic has accelerated the gig economy and made every boy and girl next door who decided to build a community, huge brands, and forces to reckon with. We have periodically used mom bloggers and influencers to promote our products. This helps us increase our audience over time on social media channels. Startups need not look for celebrities to start their influencer campaigns. Look at who your end consumer is and see if there are any micro-influencers in that space. There are several influencer marketing companies these days and if you Google them, you can try and engage a few to see if they help enhance your marketing mix. Understand that you should not, as always, expect immediate sales. Send samples to the influencers, let them use it and then post about it. This way the posts though sponsored would be more authentic. Consumers are smart and see through blatant promotions. People might buy your product once, but if there is more hype than substance be ready to lose not one but many customers through bad word-of-mouth.

I am sure your company has a blog, and you are on LinkedIn. But with the clutter, you need the help of a good SEO specialist to stand out and be found. LinkedIn has become a great tool to build your personal brand, and this is a place where you should be posting relevant content regularly. While you might not be in the B2B space, never forget that even professionals are your consumers. Being active on Instagram and Facebook too puts your brand out to your connections. I must confess that I am very bad at this Facebook and Instagram piece and rely on my social media team to keep our brand out there. Dig deep into what your brand means for your consumers and look for influencers who don't cost an arm and a leg but deliver immense value when you engage many such influencers over longer periods of time.

* * * * *

Test and Continuously Improve Products. Recall and Take Ownership When There is a Problem

You must be thinking I am crazy and contradicting myself because I said the product isn't everything earlier. Wait and hear me out. While the product isn't everything, it is and will always be your first and most important part of the marketing mix. Without the product delivering on its promise, you can't even begin building a brand that consumers love and trust.

As I type this, I found a small fragrance variation in the Bril Liquid detergent while I did the sniff test before pouring a cap-full into the washing machine. As soon as I noticed this, I went down to get a sachet and bottle from the previous batch which I always keep at home to check if I had Covid 😅, or whether there was a noticeable variation. Voila, there was a marginal variation, and I immediately took action to intimate the factory, though no consumer would have ever noticed it, and it had nothing to do with the efficacy of the product. But over and above regular lab-tests and QC, leaders must be obsessive over quality and consistency of their brand's promise to the consumer. It is not what gets noticed, but it is about making products that you yourself are happy with, proud of and love using. At Bril, we make products for ourselves first and then the consumers.

No company is perfect and in our 60-year history we have had product complaints, manufacturing defects and recalls too. Once for example, the factory mixed the dye for fountain pens with the one for stamp pad inks. The batch wrongly got despatched before the QC results came in because it was peak school season! In two weeks when it reached the consumer through the supply chain, complaints started coming in about the fountain pen ink not writing properly. As soon as I got to know this, I got my team to recall the entire batch and replace it with another batch that was ok. In these cases, the cost of not taking action is way higher than the short-term loss of recalling and replacing the product to maintain consumer trust in the brand. Similar cases have happened with almost every company that has been in existence for several decades. Car manufacturers like Toyota, Maruti, Honda have recalled some cars for parts replacements and proactively managed their brand's reputation. Poorly managed instances are the Pratt & Whitney engine problem that grounded several of their customers' aircrafts including Indian airlines like Indigo and other International Airlines for several months to years. Boeing 737-8 Max planes were grounded worldwide for over 2 years after two planes (Ethiopian and Lion Air) crashed killing 346 passengers due to a fault in the flight control system. Boeing's was a case of serious negligence that damaged its reputation and brand image badly, because the company did nothing proactively and had to be forced by Aviation Authorities to ground the planes after precious lives were lost, to fix the faulty software and train pilots before giving them permission to fly again. But the delay in acting cost precious lives to be lost and severely eroding Boeing's brand equity and trust amongst flyers for many years. This also reflected in its share price and eroded shareholder-value.

While the above are case studies from different industries, one of the biggest case studies in well-managed brand recoveries was the Johnson & Johnson Tylenol case. 5 deaths occurred one after another due to cyanide poisoned Tylenol capsules. The company recalled more than 30 million bottles and it cost them more than $100 million. After extensive testing and investigation, it was evident that the poisoning had not happened in any J&J facility or warehouses, it had happened by tampering bottles on store shelves. James Burke the CEO in 1982 when this happened immediately got his team into action to make tamper-proof bottles. Once ready the company took out an advertising Blitz communicating the poisonings as an act of terrorism and that now Tylenol was even safer due to the tamper-proof bottles. He also opened up telephone lines for anyone to call in and speak to J&J representatives to get a free bottle of Tylenol. Phones started ringing continuously with people calling in J&J and thanking them for putting people before profits. Tylenol went from 37% pre murders to 7% post murders and back to 30% market share after the trust recovery exercise, within 1 year. Such is the impact of intimate leadership!

So, summing up, test and improve products and packaging continuously and take ownership and put the customer first when something goes wrong.

* * * * *

My Sales Managers and I Fight a Good Fight, But in an Egoless Manner

Sales was and is my first focus area in business, as it is the lifeblood of any business. Most people confuse sales with marketing and the words are used interchangeably. Make no mistake, sales is ultimate closure and marketing helps achieve that, profitably. So, while marketing satisfies needs profitably, no organization can survive unless the purchase or sale is closed repeatedly, increasing the value per customer, and increasing the number of customers who fulfil their needs by buying the company's products / services. We at Bril are in the broad Fast Moving Consumer Goods (FMCG) space (Stationery, Home Care and Baby and Children's Products) and here sales teams play a pivotal role to the business. Their daily calls to retail outlets and sales makes or breaks an organization even today, in a country like India.

I have daily calls with my sales managers to get an update on the plan for the day and what happened the previous day. My relationship with my key sales managers is akin to that of good friends who can say anything to each other. While we have deep personal bonds, when we talk business, it is absolute no-nonsense straight talk. We have a clear understanding that our personal bonds happened because we have come together to fulfil the organization's mission and vision.

The biggest example of a huge difference of opinion was when I called my Kerala Regional Sales Manager and told him that overnight, we were moving to a 100% advance payment system company wide. While I spoke to both Sakthivel my TN Regional Sales Manager and Balasubramanyam (Balu), my Kerala Sales Manager, I called Balu first as I knew the difficulty he would face in Kerala. In a credit-riddled industry like FMCG, my manager thought I was crazy. The 'days receivable' (Receivables/Sales per day) in Kerala like in other states were beginning to mount and I had decided to move to a 100% advance payment system company wide. This was decided after an experiment thanks to a manager by the name Krishna Deshpande had worked well in Karnataka. Kerala is known for its distributor unions and companies could face complete loss of business. So, my manager Balasubramanyam (Balu) was right in being apprehensive. However, I had made up my mind and we had a huge fight for the future of the business. The important thing was that we both knew that we wanted the best for Bril. I told him to sleep over it and call me the next day. He called me at 7 am next morning and said, "Let's Do It". While there was a lot of bickering and noise from the market, my manager and I personally spoke to key distributors and told them that this was a company-wide decision and nothing to do with their business or their track-record with payments. The team also explained that this was good for them (the distributors) as this was the time that many stationery companies were dumping stock to show sales and burdening the distributors. We told them that they could buy and hold just one month stock and we would never dump. We told them that in the long run they would benefit. As luck would have it, GST came, and several companies couldn't recover a lot of receivables for dumped stock and accounting for returned unpaid stock became a big challenge. Distributors came back to tell us that they were very happy that we hadn't dumped stock, and we had an advance payment system, because with other companies they worked with, there was no clarity at that point if they could take VAT credits against GST payable. While these issues got sorted out by the Government later, and VAT credits were allowed to be set off against GST Payable, several unregistered dealers lost money as they had too much input credit in VAT and didn't have the wherewithal to make the claims, so they just booked the losses.

Intimate leadership is the ability to take tough calls without hampering relationships internally and externally. It's a very thin line between fighting for the organization and getting personal. So, building that underlying understanding that it is never personal into the organizational culture is crucial.

* * * * *

Everybody is a Salesman

Every time I come across people in any profession who say, 'money is not important' and 'I am not the sales type', I cringe. This mindset will get you nowhere in entrepreneurship or any leadership role. In fact, I would go on to say that we are all salesmen and are constantly selling something or the other. In an interview, are you not selling yourself? Imagine saying I am not the sales type in an interview. Doesn't it sound absurd? Every business has vendors/suppliers and customers, and on a daily basis we have to negotiate and sell value-propositions to get the best deals from Vendors and offer maximum value to our customers. Sales is actually a service we do to our customers and consumers. Whenever people think sales, they think of the pushy Eureka Forbes salesman, the sleazy used car salesman or a door-to-door salesman who sells you stuff you don't need. However, without being in sales, nobody is in business. No matter what your role is, you will have to sell yourself, your products, your brand's value proposition, your ideas and more to various stakeholders. While middle class values are fantastic and I personally follow them, there is this dangerous middle-class mindset that says money is bad or evil. This mindset makes people who possess it become overly critical of anyone who has money or makes money. It is actually an inferiority complex masked as a superiority complex and hinders the growth of the person.

Can you imagine selling a BMW with that kind of mindset? No, because you believe that it is a waste of money at your core. Whether you are just starting off in a corporate job or are starting your own company, you should understand that you have to get over any limiting beliefs. If you must sell anything, you first have to have the faith in yourself and the value of what you are selling in the life of the consumer. I tell my salesmen that just because they feel something is too expensive based on their upbringing, affordability, and circumstances, it doesn't mean it is expensive for everyone. Price and discretionary spends are subjective and as leaders we must first have an open and non-judgmental understanding of this. When in business we must understand at our very core that what we are doing for the customer is service – solving a problem, satisfying a need, or fulfilling an aspirational desire for him/her.

Ok so you say 'I am in HR why do I need sales'. Imagine you are setting a culture for your team. How would you sell it to your team? 'What about finance? I surely don't need sales, right?' How would you sell the budget for say marketing to your leadership? What about operations? Well, how would you sell a production optimization to your boss to save costs for the company? Trust me, every act of ours is sales. We are selling ideas or products or concepts day in and day out. So please do yourself a favour and understand that we are all in sales whether we like it or not. The next time you buy a soap, think of, and thank the salesman who took the order and got it delivered to the shop by the distributor. What if you buy on Amazon nobody sold the product to you right? No, the organization's marketing team has been selling you their ideas which have resonated with you and hence you are making the final purchase decision out of all the available choices you have. So, if you run your business and hate sales, I am sorry to say that you will have to develop that skill, or you should get a co-founder who is very good at it while you probably focus on tech. Even in Tech, if you are a leader, you need to sell your ideas to the team. Sales is everywhere and we are all in sales!

* * * * *

Never Ignore the Power of Feet on The Street

My journey with Bril started by visiting markets with front-line salesmen, to understand first-hand what trade and consumers want. I did this continuously for many years and continue to do it whenever I get the time. There is no better joy than seeing one's brand on the shelves of retail outlets and there is no bigger blow to the ego than when one's product is rejected in your face by wholesalers and retailers. I still make it a point to visit markets whenever I get time, but I have limited time. So, to substitute this, I am constantly in touch with my sales managers and even frontline salesmen through WhatsApp groups every single day. I analyse my salesmen's performance on our sales app and ask them to share photos of well-stocked shops for our social media channels. I get a feel of what is moving and what is not and where the salesmen are putting in their efforts or not. I ask my salesmen to share videos and photos of shops and product placement in the sales group so I can see multiple markets without being there physically. All my salesmen have direct access to me if they need to keep me posted on any competitor activity or changing consumer behaviours. No matter how much automation and data we have for social listening and analysing buyer behaviour, nothing, in my opinion beats direct inputs from real people hitting the markets every day. If you are a D2C founder you might ask me how feet on the street will help you. I am a firm believer in the power of being Omni Channel as you have to be everywhere your customers are. Even if you are just starting off as a purely online brand, recruit 1-2 people to visit stores that carry competitor products or even to analyse form competition. What is form competition? Form competition is competition from a totally different product that solves the same or similar problem for your consumer. For example, let me take the example of my brand Bril itself. Though the ball point pen was invented by Jon J Loud way back in 1888, it was not until Milton Reynolds invented the ballpoint pen named after him and launched it in New York in October 1945 did it catch the fancy of consumers. It came much later in the 1980s to India, but its real impact for writing ink sales wasn't felt till 1990s. While my father to his credit moved quickly and launched and sold a lot of ball point pens called Bril Primo Dx in the 90s and early 2000s, the rapid change in writing technology was something that we could just not keep up with. The moulds were very expensive, and a model could be a hit or a miss and every rupee invested in the mould would go down the tube, if a model failed. We did have a few of those experiences too. So, it wasn't another fountain pen ink brand that shook our foundation back in the day, it was a totally different pen that needed a totally different ink! While we have subsequently launched and sell great liquid fluid ball point pens, I can say it is purely God's grace and a miracle that we survived that onslaught and are still in business. This is form competition at its best or worst depending on how you look at it. The camera film roll industry would have never thought that the digital camera would change the photography landscape so drastically.

The smartphone disrupted digital cameras, feature phones, entertainment, banking, and several other industries! So, your feet on the street should start reporting direct and form competition and changes in consumer behaviour regularly, whether you are selling to brick and mortar stores or not. In today's ever-changing world, the changes are even more rapid, and we must run to stay at the same place, else the rug will get pulled off from beneath our feet. I cannot stress enough the importance of flexibility and the ability to adapt in today's marketplace. Don't be paranoid, enjoy the ride, but don't tell me I didn't warn you that this is one of the scariest roller coasters!

* * * * *

How We Have the Liberty to Start and Grow Products We Love, Slowly

Most funded start-ups today are in a hurry. A mad hurry to scale, disrupt and break things, so the investors and founders can get an exit. What I write about is the exact opposite of that. How being slow like the tortoise can build a solid foundation for a multi-generational profitable business. While I am not averse to exits in-case of the unpredictability of life and business or the next generation not being interested / inability to professionalize, I believe in thinking and having the intent to build organizations that can stand the test of time and build household brands. So, the way we look at product launches is to launch quickly, test and kill or test and scale (if successful). We have over the years had a success rate of around 20%. So, if we launch 5 products, 1 succeeds and 4 fail. This is a classic way of failing fast and failing forward. We never manufacture our own products when we first launch because the CAPEX (Capital Expenditure) is too much, and it forces you to persist with products even if there is no product-market-fit. With sub-contracted manufacturing we can get relatively smaller runs manufactured and test the market before we make any significant investments or continue to work with the same factory if they are a good partner. So, the important thing is to find a gap in the market and be quick to launch and scale, or bite the bullet and kill the product. There is no room for ego in business. It's very important to train your teams to recognize stars and duds quickly, so bad launches don't drain your organization too much before you pull them out. At the same time allocating capital for the star products with higher margins will help you stay in business for longer. The hardest part in an ever-changing world is to keep running and stay in business for the long-haul.

* * * * *

What is our Vision and How Should You Think About a Vision for your Organization?

Bril's Vision

To Be India's best and most loved 100% Indian consumer products brand, that helps Make Living Fun™ for its consumers and all stakeholders.

Bril's Vision and Mission have evolved after several years of deliberation and course correction.

Leading legendary brands across the world, that have added value and continue to add value for decades and even centuries are those that have a clear vision.

So, the Vision for an organization is the big picture of where you as an organization are headed and where you want to be in the years to come. So, what's your organization's Vision? Think about how your consumers would be 5, 10 or even 50 years down the line. Which business are you really in? A Vision should be a big dream of where you wish to be in future. Make sure you are not too narrowly focussed as single product visions seldom last for more than 5 years these days. If you see Bril's Vision, you will see that there will always be consumer products and no matter how the products are distributed, consumers will always need daily essential products in some form or the other to bathe, brush, clean their homes, wash their clothes, take some notes etc. So, the Vision accommodates the fact that along the way consumer behaviours may change and the consumer products may change (we don't narrowly define consumer products in the Vision statement), but the Vision doesn't have to change – it can merely be expanded if we wish to cater to more geographies in future.

* * * * *

How Our Mantra and Mission Came about and How It Positively Impacted Team Performance

Bril's Mantra

Make Living Fun™

Bril's Mission

To Make Living Fun™ for everyone through world-class products and service.

* * * * *

Why do We Exist, Why Do You Exist?

Bril exists to fulfil its mission – To Make Living Fun for Everyone through World-Class Products and Service. So 'Make Living Fun' is its mantra and tag line. This mission and mantra came about from a Sanskrit sloka 'Loka Samastha Sukhino Bhavantu' which means, let all creatures be free and happy and let my thoughts and actions in this birth contribute to their freedom and happiness in some way. So, at Bril every team member, when they join are groomed by their manager to imbibe this mantra and mission and carry it out to Make Living Fun for their co-workers, customers, consumers, and all stakeholders while working with the highest level of ethics and the Nishkama Karma value system.

While I am not a brand purpose advocate, because I believe customers buy brands to fulfil their needs (which may include core needs / status or aspirational needs / self-actualization needs etc) or solve their problems, I believe it is very important for your teams to know why they exist, and why they have come together (You could call this purpose if you relate better to it). The Vision, Mission, Mantra, and Value System bind people from varied backgrounds together to achieve a common goal, which is larger than any individual. It is only when the collective, streamlined execution of the mission, in line with the values espoused takes place, can the Vision be achieved by any brand and organization.

* * * * *

Bril's Nishkama Karma Value System

Bril's Value System

The age-old Indian philosophy of Nishkama Karma

We work to fulfil our mission daily by adopting the age-old Indian philosophy of Nishkama Karma. Our entire team is trained to look at work as a duty and we carry out our duty without hankering after rewards as stated in the Bhagavad Gita. Duty for the sake of duty without hankering after rewards with other people's benefits in mind helps us Make Living Fun™ for Everyone and for ourselves as a by-product!

At Bril every team member is taught and practices the Nishkama Karma Value System. What is this value system? This is the core teaching of the Bhagavad Gita where Lord Krishna Tells Arjuna to focus and carry out the task at hand without worrying about the outcome. So, this is precisely what we teach every employee. For example, if a salesman has a lead, his duty is to vet the lead, nurture it and follow it up with all his heart. The final sales closure may or may not happen even for the best of salespeople at times and so if we establish that the efforts and follow-up have happened it is ok to lose a few deals. So, the Nishkama Karma philosophy runs deeply through the core culture of the organization where every team member goes out of their way to do their duty without hankering after rewards and recognition, and more importantly with other stakeholders' benefits in mind. They know that good work gets recognized sooner than later and results come as a by-product of fulfilling one's duties and beyond. All this said, we believe in doing anything we do without compromising on ethics.

Now let us just look at some examples of Vision, Mission, and Values from some exceptional, legendary, and timeless brands so you can gain inspiration to work on framing your Startup's / Organization's Vision, Mission, and Values. Please note that some of the companies don't have a vision statement and hence not mentioned below.

Nike:

Mission: *"Bring Inspiration and Innovation to every athlete in the world."*

Tag Line: Just Do It

Nike strikes an emotional chord by being the biggest advocate of excellence in sport. Nike empowers every child, adult, and aspiring athlete / sportsperson to Just Do It. One needn't be an aspiring athlete but just be on a mission to lose weight or work out every day and Nike strikes that chord of making the consumer take action and Just Do It. Over the years, Nike has sponsored greats like Michael Jordan, Tiger Woods, Roger Federer and more across sports to make the brand super-aspirational for every kid dreaming about becoming like their sports heroes. Now NIKE also has the up-and-coming next gen in tennis, Alcarez who beat Djokovic in the 2023 Wimbledon endorsing them. NIKE has transformed a commodity like a shoe into an aspirational emotion!

Apple:

Vision: "To make the best products on earth and to leave the world better than we found it."

Mission: "To bring the best user experience to customers through innovative hardware, software, and services."

Tag Line: Think Different

Apple Values

- Accessibility.
- Education.
- Racial Equity and Justice.

Apple clearly exists to empower and improve the lives of those who believe they are different and do not follow the herd. Apple's vision, mission and tag line clearly indicate its commitment to superior design and user-experience that will make the products and services an intimate part of their consumers' lives.

In his now famous speech to Apple employees upon his return, Steve Jobs talks about how he was inspired by Nike which created a phenomenal brand while producing a shoe which is a commodity. He says, Nike honours great athletes and they honour great athletics. Nike never speaks about their product and yet make you aspire to be in a pair. So, Apple's core Values he goes on to say should never change. Apple at its core believes that **'People with passion change the world for**

the better. And the people who are crazy enough to think they can change the world are the ones who do.' These values subtly yet clearly define who Apple's employees, customers and stakeholders at their core are. They are the misfits, dreamers, and those that Think Different and know they can change the world and make it a better place. The now famous ad campaign he then goes on to play talks about all those crazy people who thought different and actually changed the world for the better. So, this core value is so emotional that it has moved people for decades and consumers have become raving fans and advocates of Apple and its products.

TATA:

Vision

To be globally significant in each of our chosen businesses by 2025.

Mission

To be the most reliable global network for customers and suppliers, that delivers value through products and services. To be a responsible value creator for all our stakeholders.

Values

Pioneering

We will be bold and agile, courageously taking on challenges, using deep customer insight to develop innovative solutions.

Integrity

We will be fair, honest, transparent and ethical in our conduct; everything we do must stand the test of public scrutiny.

Excellence

We will be passionate about achieving the highest standards of quality, always promoting meritocracy.

Unity

We will invest in our people and partners, enable continuous learning, and build caring and collaborative relationships based on trust and mutual respect.

Responsibility

We will integrate environmental and social principles in our businesses, ensuring that what comes from the people goes back to the people many times over.

Microsoft:

Mission:

Our mission is to empower every person and every organization on the planet to achieve more.

Values:

Respect

Integrity

Accountability

Marico:

Marico has a simple yet very powerful Value System and that's it.

It is – Make A Difference.

Only when you're empowered with freedom and opportunity do you rise above the task at hand and take complete ownership to make a difference.

This is like their tag line, mission, and values. Whether it is their employees or brands, they exist to make a difference.

Asian Paints:

Vision

We want to be an innovative, agile, and responsive world class research and technology organisation that's aligned to future customer needs and catalyses the growth of the company across existing and future businesses.

Mission

To provide paints as per market demand, ensuring desired level and quality of customer service, continued availability of the right product mix of right quality at the right time.

The above Vision, Mission and Value statements have been shared from respective company websites, only for purposes of inspiration. You should sit with your team and write your company's. It should be something that your gut says, yes to and excites you and your team to go after what you collectively wish to achieve.

* * * * *

Dealing With Heritage Issues and Implementing Change for Sustenance and Growth

People dealing with family businesses will relate to this chapter and get an idea as to how they can gain credibility with different stakeholders in their company.

When I first joined my family business Bril back in 2002, it was not smooth sailing. One would think that the owner's son would get a warm welcome from everyone. This is so not true as my business had run for more than 38 years before I joined and had very senior (in age and experience) employees and heritage trade relationships. The year was 2002 when I first joined the company and started by visiting the markets to meet super-stockists and distributors. When I joined, we were more dependent on our trade partners as we had just 2-3 salesmen for the 4 states we operated in. When I went in, I could immediately sense the unease by some of the senior trade partners, as I was asking many questions. They had become used to owning their territory with just targets being fixed by the company. My objective from day one was to make Bril a consumer products brand from just having ink and a few stationery product SKUs. When I communicated this to the trade partners, some point-blank told me that only ink will sell, others humoured me but made it clear that we were an ink company. As inexperienced as

I was, I was burning inside, but couldn't show my displeasure. Little did I know that the journey of entrepreneurship means getting prepared for many blows to one's ego. When I visited wholesale and retail with some new stationery products, one of them literally threw it back at me saying they would buy only Bril Ink! What made this worse was employees within my organization believed that only ink was 'our' product and stationery products were mere attachments, or worse, distractions. Over the years, with a lot of patience, blood sweat, tears, and persistence I started communicating with employees and trade partners that we were Bril and not Bril Ink. Any small change I made or when managers recruited by me set sales targets for 'other items' as stationery products were disparagingly called, trade partners would call my father to complain and say the targets were unachievable. My father would gently let them know that I was in-charge, and it was important for the organization to reduce its dependence on fountain pen inks (while also increasing sales of fountain pen inks and fountain pens) as the world was changing to ball point pens and becoming a stationery / consumer products brand was the way to go. Over the years, with experience, I stopped getting angry and realized that their behaviour was a result of their own fear and personal short-term needs. They would sell what gave them most profits and volumes, with the least amount of effort. So, whether it was the older employees or trade partners, for them it was self-preservation and nothing more. They didn't care about the bigger picture because change was hard work and scary. By around 2012, I had recruited a full-fledged field force, but the managers had to fight internally and externally to even get basic reports. Every quarter I would write to my trade partners and coax them of the importance of sharing their stock positions and movement analysis with the company. In this process, we took the tough decision of removing two old-time super-stockists. When this happened, surprisingly the others woke up and started cooperating, because they realized that not cooperating would be detrimental to their business. So intimate leadership is not trying to please everyone but doing what's best for the organization and all stakeholders. In this case the trade partners were causing damage by not-cooperating and preventing the organization's growth. They would refuse to supply stationery product orders taken by the salesmen and only sell ink to their regular retail and wholesale outlets. Word spread that I was going to ruin the business and phone calls went to my father and all old-time employees (very good and loyal people). But my father, me and the new sales team stood strong in our conviction that this was best for everyone.

The major turnaround happened when I identified Sakthivel who was a sales representative and made him Area Sales Manager in 2013 (and subsequently Regional Sales Manager) for Tamil Nadu. He was and is till today super hardworking and a great no-nonsense people-person. He works the market, gets business for all trade partners and makes sure they follow all SOPs (Standard Operating Procedures) of the organization. Today, by God's grace and the efforts of Sakthi and his team, all trade partners sell every single product in our portfolio and have seen their revenues and profits grow. As results started coming in, I gained credibility in the ecosystem, and employees (old and new) and trade partners started taking my decisions seriously. So, even if it is your family business, nothing will work unless you gain credibility and make people realize that you have the organization's and their best interests in mind.

Also, if you are joining your family business, start by working on the shop floor, visit the markets, learn the ropes from the ground-level. Interact with senior employees, ask for their guidance and learn from them so they start trusting you.

* * * * *

How We Identify and Promote People and How you Should do It?

If my memory is right, the year was 2012 and we had just launched BrilSlate, an Android tablet, primarily to sell to and through our independent home-based resellers. In hindsight I realize it was the stupidest move I have made in my 21-year career with Bril. Why would a fast-moving consumer-products company dabble in electronic products? It was a moment of madness and me losing focus and getting carried away by the shiny new object that was android tablets back in the day. This launch however did one good thing. We as an organization were clueless about tech and were just importing these branded Android tablets from China and reselling them. The tablets were great, and we sold a few, but we had big issues with servicing the tablets under warranty. It was during this time that Sakthivel, who was then a front-line sales representative, rose to the occasion to take charge. Through pure passion for technology, he managed to partner with a service organization and personally managed customer needs and servicing requests like a true leader. I was keenly observing this frontline stationery salesman, who couldn't speak English fluently handle complex technical issues that cropped up with the BrilSlate tablets by liaising between the servicing team in the organization he helped us partner with and the customer. While my sanity and focus on fast moving consumer products returned and we killed the BrilSlate forever, I had found a true leader. This WAS THE BEST OUTCOME from a failed product launch. Once I noticed him, I realized that he was super data-obsessed and was doing his boss's job too, for a few years. So, I made Sakthi the Area Sales Manager for Tamil Nadu for our core business. Sakthi is a rare leader who becomes a salesman in the market, a manager in meetings, a people leader daily, a coach, mentor, learner, and a super passionate brand-advocate! What made this even better was that this happened at the same time I took charge from the CEO who I had to let go off. It was a period of great instability for the organization which I will explain in more detail in the next chapter.

In your company, always keep your eyes open to find leaders emerge. Do not wait to promote people or hire for a post from outside when you see passion and excellence in action. Do not worry about hierarchy if you see an employee in the lowest-rung take initiative beyond his/her call of duty. Just promote them and recognize their great leadership beyond their title/position. Look for people who everyone respects, for their skill and nature. Avoid people pleasers because they seldom make good leaders. Good leaders are those who are friends with people outside of the work environment but don't think twice before direct confrontation, if necessary, in the workplace. They are people who do not remember arguments and put their ego aside and look only at the situation on hand. These are gems that you as an owner/founder/director/leader should be able to intuitively identify and promote for the benefit of your organization.

* * * * *

Change of Product, Packaging or Product Design for the Sake of Change Is Disastrous

We have two very successful Geometry Box brands namely Bril Geomate Smart and Bril Geomate DX catering to the mass market and slightly premium segments. In 2013, almost all of our competitors were changing their designs to make their packaging more attractive. When I spoke to the owner of our OEM factory, he insisted that we too change our design, as our design was dated. I made the mistake of hiring a very good freelance designer, who according to me came up with a beautiful, novel design that gave our Geometry boxes a kaleidoscope effect. While I was super thrilled with the new design, that school season saw sales of our Geometry boxes dip by 50%! Yes, I had just not sensed the pulse of the market! I quickly bit the bullet and went back to the old design elements with minor changes within 6 months and lo sales started picking up again. To their credit, the sales teams told me that the market had rejected the design. Though at first I asked them to push harder and see if we could make inroads, I had to sooner than later swallow my ego, accept my mistake, and roll back to the old design theme and elements that the market loved. This taught me a critical lesson of understanding my consumers and their preferences intimately before making any major design change. While I could have changed the design a bit, I should have kept the much loved 100% yellow background and geometry box parts elements similar to the old design. This I did do, but after taking a hit on sales. While competitors maybe doing all sorts of things, we should realize what consumers love about our brand and not deviate from what makes them identify our brand uniquely.

A classic case study of even market research failing, is that of the New Coke flavour launch in 1985. Blind tasting of a sample of over 200000 consumers with a budget of &4 million showed that majority of the respondents loved the taste of New Coke over the Old one. I have used my own thoughts and excerpts from a well-written version from history.com, of this famous case study of how we as leaders and marketers must never underestimate the emotional connect that consumers have with a classic brand, even if research and consumer-taste-preferences tells us otherwise.

If it ain't broke, don't fix it.

The time-tested adage appears to be the lesson from Coca-Cola's disastrous introduction of "New Coke." Except in 1985, Coca-Cola indeed thought its signature brand was broken.

Although Coca-Cola remained the world's best-selling soft drink, rival Pepsi-Cola continued to gain market share in the 1970s and early 1980s, thanks in part to its aggressive "Pepsi Challenge" campaign in which consumers taking blind taste tests were surprised to learn they preferred the flavour of Pepsi. To the shock of Coca-Cola, internal taste tests yielded the same results. Company executives grew convinced that its soda's taste—not its rival's advertisements targeting the

"Pepsi Generation"—was the reason for its declining market share.

Since its introduction in 1886, Coca-Cola's secret recipe had been tweaked several times—such as when changing sweeteners from cane sugar to beet sugar to corn syrup—but its taste had remained constant. While the company was developing the unique formula for Diet Coke, which was introduced in 1982, it found in top-secret taste tests that a sweeter version of the concoction beat not only Pepsi but the classic version of Coke. Executives decided to make a risky change.

Coca-Cola bets everything on New Coke

On April 23, 1985, Coca-Cola Company chairman and CEO Roberto Goizueta stepped before the press gathered at New York City's Lincoln Center to introduce the new formula, which he declared to be "smoother, rounder, yet bolder—a more harmonious flavour." The press, however, said what Goizueta couldn't admit: New Coke tasted sweeter and more like Pepsi.

Had it been an opera, the Lincoln Center performance would have been a tragedy to devoted fans of Coke's original formula. Rather than divide its market share between two sugar sodas, Coca-Cola discontinued its 99-year classic recipe and locked Formula 7x away in an Atlanta bank vault with the intention that it never again see the light of day.

"Some may choose to call this the boldest single marketing move in the history of the packaged-goods business," Goizueta said. "We simply call it the surest move ever made."

Coca-Cola president Donald Keough echoed the certainty: "I've never been as confident about a decision as I am about the one we're announcing today."

New Coke falls flat.

While Goizueta and Keough toasted each other with cans of New Coke, the news was already beginning to fall flat. On the New York Stock Exchange, shares of Coca-Cola dropped, while those of its rival rose. Pepsi gave its employees the day off and declared victory in full-page newspaper advertisements that boasted, "After 87 years of going at it eyeball to eyeball, the other guy just blinked."

New Coke left a bitter taste in the mouths of the company's loyal customers. Within weeks of the announcement, the company was fielding 5,000 angry phone calls a day. By June, that number grew to 8,000 calls a day, a volume that forced the company to hire extra operators. "I don't think I'd be more upset if you were to burn the flag in our front yard," one disgruntled drinker wrote to company headquarters. At protests staged by grassroots groups such as "Old Cola Drinkers of America," consumers poured the contents of New Coke bottles into sewer drains. One Seattle consumer even filed suit against the company to force it to provide the old drink.

The outrage caught Coca-Cola executives by surprise. They had hardly made a rash decision unsupported by data. After all, they had performed 190,000 blind taste tests on U.S. and Canadian consumers. The problem, though, is that the company had underestimated loyal drinkers' emotional attachments to the brand. Never did its market research testers ask subjects how they would feel if the new formula replaced the old one.

Coca-Cola Classic returns

Seventy-nine days after their initial announcement, Coca-Cola executives once again held a press conference on July 11, 1985—this time to announce a *mea culpa* and the return of the original formula, which hardly had time to gather dust in its Atlanta bank vault, under the label "Coca-Cola Classic." "Our boss is the consumer," Keough said. "We want them to know we're really sorry." The news was so momentous that television networks broke into normal programming with special reports.

Coca-Cola Classic quickly outsold New Coke and within a few months had returned to its position as the top-selling sugar cola, ahead of Pepsi. The company rebranded the new formula "Coke II" in 1990 before it was eventually abandoned in 2002. In spite of the blowback, Coca-Cola emerged from the fiasco with its market position actually strengthened as consumers rediscovered their attachment to the iconic brand. (Moreover, in 2019, Coca-Cola actually re-released a very limited run of New Coke.)

"The simple fact is that all the time and money and skill poured into consumer research on the new Coca-Cola could not measure or reveal the deep and abiding emotional attachment to original Coca-Cola felt by so many people," Keough admitted. The blunder was so colossal that some thought it must have been an intentional marketing gimmick. "Some cynics say that we planned the whole thing," Keough said. "The truth is we're not that dumb and we're not that smart."*

Now rebranding Facebook to Meta and pouring billions into the Metaverse project may or may not yield desired results. Only time will tell if Mark Zuckerberg made a very costly mistake or was a true visionary.

*Quotes taken from history.com. See references.

* * * * *

So, What Makes Consumers So Passionate About 'Their Coke'? – It's Biochemistry at Work!

Coca-Cola today has a market capitalization of USD 263.2 Billion as I write this. How did the company make people world-over drink so much of its commoditized sugar water with some cola and caffeine for 131 years?

100 MIT students were put through MRI machines only to understand why Coke is a preferred brand! On a hot summer day, 100 students at the Massachusetts Institute, USA were given a can of Coke and a can of Pepsi each. And were asked to evaluate the taste. The important thing is that they were blindfolded. The result was almost identical - 51 or so said Coke tasted better and 49 or so said Pepsi tasted better.

Now the same 100 students were given another can of Coke and Pepsi each and were again asked to evaluate the taste. This time their eyes were open. Guess what?

Close to 70 percent said Coke tasted better and only about 20 per cent said Pepsi tasted better.

The researchers were totally shocked.

To understand the reason, they put these 100 students through brain imaging and MRI scans again while they saw and sipped Coca Cola and Pepsi. They did a brain mapping study and what they found was astonishing.

There is something called the Ventromedial Prefrontal Cortex (VPFC) in our brains which is responsible for emotions. When people were blindfolded, this was activated for both Coke and Pepsi, especially due to the sugar content of the drinks.

But when people SAW Coke and tasted it, something else happened.

There is the Dorsolateral Prefrontal Cortex (DLPFC) that is responsible for higher functions such as memory and associations in the frontal part of our brains. Coke managed to stir this too because of all the consistent emotional associations the brand had done over the 100-odd years!

Additionally, there is a dopamine (the pleasure chemical) link that connects the front part of the brain to the pleasure centres. When people SAW and tasted Coke, all the associations the brand had created, stirred this dopamine link thereby releasing Dopamine in their brains. Unbelievable right? Hormone secretions making someone say Coke tastes better even if there is no logical reason for the response!

Emotions are biochemistry and hence Brand Creation is biochemistry! Recognising what it is that triggers the special parts of the brain to create a wedge and create that intimacy with the consumer is the art and science of building great brands.

* * * * *

How Indra Nooyi and Shiv Shivakumar Energized PepsiCo

While PepsiCo has always been a close second to Coca Cola globally in the beverages category, Indra Nooyi was instrumental in making PepsiCo a formidable snacks and beverages company that is today much larger than coco-cola in terms of revenues (USD 90.14 Billion Pepsi Vs USD 43.49 Billion Coca Cola). Nooyi was the first woman and immigrant to run a Fortune 50 company when she became Chairman and CEO of PepsiCo global in 2006. She has consistently ranked among the world's 100 most powerful women. In 2014, she was ranked at number 13 on the Forbes list of The World's 100 Most Powerful Women and was ranked the second most powerful woman on the Fortune list in 2015 and 2017. Nooyi joined PepsiCo in 1994 and had an almost immediate influence on the company's strategic direction. An astute tactician, Nooyi oversaw a number of key restructurings during her first years with the company: in 1997, Pepsi elected to spin off its Pizza Hut, KFC, and Taco Bell restaurants for $4.5bn. The company used the proceeds of the sale to slash its $8.5bn debt mountain by more than half, a move that also allowed the business to accelerate its share buyback strategy, giving it the financial flexibility to invest in further business development. The following year Indra Nooyi purchased Tropicana for $3.3 Billion to take on Coca-Cola's Minute Maid in the non-fizzy fruit beverages category. Nooyi also went on to acquire Quaker for $13.4 Billion which gave PepsiCo access to healthy snacks and Gatorade in beverages. Nooyi's consumer intimacy was seen clearly when she started navigating PepsiCo to a 'more healthy' option for consumers. Back in the day it was frowned upon, but today, in hindsight we know it was the right thing for her to do. Nooyi classified the products into three distinct categories 'fun for you' (such as potato chips and regular soda), 'better for you' (diet or low-fat versions of snacks and fizzy drinks), and 'good for you' (Quaker Oatmeal). This is an area, in my opinion that Coca Cola has done very little despite dominating the cola and fizzy drinks category. Indra Nooyi's leadership has hence been recognized as steering a brand towards what is good for consumers. As I always say, we should always do what is best for us and our families for our consumers also. While an occasional fizzy drink is fine, it shouldn't become a daily consumption habit. Dietary balance has been a key feature of Nooyi's strategy since day one. In 2010, she declared that Pepsi needed to be part of the solution to "one of the world's biggest public health challenges – a challenge fundamentally linked to our industry: obesity". Under her leadership, Pepsi has reduced the portion sizes of its 'fun for you' products and has delivered a marketing campaign to ensure its 'diet' products are promoted aspirationally as opposed to its full-sugar equivalents. For example, Gatorade is now marketed specifically towards athletes, rather than being advertised as an everyday recreational beverage. This required guts to do back in the day as today most CPG (Consumer Packaged Goods) F&B leaders are reacting to changing consumer buying behaviours towards more healthy options. Indra

Nooyi also did a radical design shift and made vending machines interactive like iPads getting more intimate with consumers who would be prompted based on their previous choices based on their IDs etc.

Both Indra Nooyi Ex Chairman and CEO PepsiCo and Shiv Shivakumar Ex Chairman and CEO PepsiCo India were amazing people leaders. Both of them IIM Calcutta alums, have truly shaped PepsiCo globally and in India respectively during their leadership tenures. In November 2013 as stated in an ET article, Shiv met Indra Nooyi in her New Jersey home. They bonded over south Indian delicacies and discussed the future of PepsiCo under Shiv who was to take charge as Chairman and CEO. Shiv started his stint by meeting all stakeholders and energized the employees about the future of the company. He firmly believed an intimate connection with his team was top priority and market share and profits would follow. Shiv travelled extensively to meet all stakeholders like customers, distributors, retailers, ad agencies and bottlers. People could reach him directly if they had any problem and he would ensure that his team solved the issue. He was and is a true intimate leader.

Shiv in an interview with Master's Union talks about how competitive advantages of today will no longer be advantages tomorrow. He has always thought of how any business he manages will make money 5 years down the line. While most international MNCs fall flat in India because they fail to understand the consumer, Shiv managed to make PepsiCo India hugely successful and profitable from a loss-making operation. Shiv did something very important for a market like India. Every time someone from an international market/

HO visited India, he would make them visit local markets and interact with trade partners, retailers, wholesalers, distributors, and consumers. This would give the senior leadership an opportunity to also interact and understand consumer behaviour, price sensitivity etc. So, decisions Shiv took would get easier buy-in from the global leaders, because now meetings would become how to grow the brand rather than who is right. He did an amazing thing to remove ego from the equation by sensitizing visitors from the global HO to local Indian realities. This was a huge learning for me personally, as this is the primary reason why so many global brands fall flat in India. India is a complex, value-conscious market and super hard to crack for any outsider.

* * * * *

Shiv's Nokia Journey

Shiv did something amazing at Nokia well before he joined PepsiCo. When he and his team realized that rural women were not buying mobile phones, they asked them why. The answer they got was that they don't need a mobile phone and they could give the Rs. 1500 to their son or daughter to study. Here is where it gets interesting, as leaders we should never take what the consumer says at face value. Consumers have aspirational desires that they do not necessarily communicate when you ask direct questions. Shiv knew this very well and his gut told him that they wanted a mobile phone, so he posed a different question. He asked them if they would buy a mobile phone if they could pay Rs. 75 per week for 25 weeks. Lo and behold, they said that would work! So, Nokia partnered with a finance partner and went to the rural market, but not a single woman bought the mobile phone. When asked why, they said, "we can buy the phone, but what about the sim card?". Shiv, in the interview candidly says even the assumption that the rural consumer would buy the phone and then go to buy a SIM card backfired! But he immediately realised what the consumer was saying was why are you not giving me the whole bundle? So that's what they did. They gave the sim card from a leading operator free and sold 2 million cell phones to rural women that year! The service provider was happy because they made money monthly from these 2 million new consumers! This is a classic way to crack the India story and only a leader like

Shiv can narrate it so beautifully. When I first met Shiv as a student at Great Lakes Institute of Management in Chennai in 2004 during my MBA, I was floored by his stories and leadership and marketing insights, and I continue to follow him on LinkedIn.

* * * * *

How I Hired a Professional and Lost that Personal Touch for a Few Years

In 2009, I had started another services organization and decided to recruit a CEO for Bril, in 2011. Without taking names, I chose a man who had helped me recruit a few managers and was a senior FMCG man. He was known to build brands and be hands on by visiting the markets and walking the talk. While recruiting him, he accepted a much lower salary than what he was getting at his previous organization, stating that he wanted to get out of the mad corporate rat race and also pursue his spirituality. Given his past experience, I didn't notice any red flag at that time. I thought, recruiting a great person would help Bril with its next phase of growth and give me the time to focus more on my new startup. Little did I know that 'professionalizing' a family business is no easy task. It took me two years to realize that I had made a BIG mistake in recruiting this person and had missed a red flag during the recruitment. This man was treating this job like lifetime employment without delivering on what was expected of him. So, he assumed he could retire here and take it easy with little or no accountability. Things really got bad when he wouldn't visit the market or attend meetings and didn't sack a person despite several ethics lapses. Though I would regularly follow-up I had to push him to do certain things. It is when I started getting calls regularly from my managers and other senior people in my organization, did I wake up to the fact that I had made a big mistake. I took full responsibility for this mistake because I hadn't read the situation properly. I had made a hiring mistake and tried to 'professionalize' prematurely. Fortunately, my startup wasn't doing great, so I wound it up and decided to double down on my first baby – Bril. In 2012, I let him go and took charge of day-to-day operations at Bril again, with 100% focus this time around.

So, is professionalizing bad? Not at all. I have utmost respect for professional leaders and their ability to scale organization. However, I had made the mistake of not building and communicating a good culture by then. While I was there, I was unknowingly building bonds with people and people were used to my working style, but I had not built that very important culture which I would have to Instill in every employee recruited. This incident happened before we had a formal culture, Vision, Mission, and Mantra. We had a deep-rooted ethics-based value-system always, and we were a typical family-business that took care of its employees well. We couldn't pay very high salaries, but we had extremely loyal and hardworking people who would stick with us and give their heart and soul for the organization. I to date thank God for giving me such great people, who take care of my organization and brand.

Companies like Marico have done a brilliant job of professionalizing their teams and attract top talent from the best B-Schools and compete with the MNCs on most parameters due to their culture of empowerment and intimate leadership styles. We all have a lot to learn from organizations like Asian Paints and Marico, that have consistently compounded shareholder value by building strong, professional teams through great organizational culture. These are two of only 7 companies that have grown their revenues at greater than 10% per annum and have had a ROCE of >15% for over 20 years straight. This is no easy achievement and has only been achieved by 7 companies in the entire publicly listed companies' space in India, as researched by Saurabh Mukherjee's Marcellus Investment Managers.

* * * * *

Beware of Employees who Bring Their Entire Team from Their Previous Organization

The CEO I had to let go off had helped me recruit two managers when he was a consultant to our company (Even before he joined our company). When he was let go off, he spread rumours about how employee-unfriendly we were and that their jobs too would go. He tried to convince pretty much every key employee to leave with him. This was a period of great unrest, and many people didn't know what the future would hold for them and whether they should leave for greener pastures based on what this man was saying. Fortunately, most senior managers knew me and my father well before this man came. They played a crucial role in convincing people that Bril was all about long-term commitment to all stakeholders including employees. Many people who were confused also called me and I gave them my word that I wanted to see people grow with the organization and that nothing had changed. This made a huge difference and barring one person who was a relatively new recruit, the entire team stayed back. While this was a difficult period, the people who stayed back have seen a great trajectory in their careers. The person who left, tells my managers till date that he made a mistake by listening to the CEO who was let go off.

After this incident I would like to tell all founders and leaders to never recruit anyone who has the habit of pulling in their entire teams with them to the company they join. This is because such people never build organizations, they just build their own careers at the cost of organizational continuity. This in fact goes totally against the intimate leadership philosophy of helping organizations thrive while allowing employees to make informed decisions to build solid, long-term careers. The managers and leaders who stayed back at Bril were those who knew they were valued at Bril and didn't get swayed by one man's personal grouse and agenda.

* * * * *

How We Moved from Quarterly to a Daily Sales Discipline and How You Can Too

Once the CEO was sacked, during a monthly sales review meeting, I felt something amiss. Like with several past meetings the sales manager reviewed the month and quarter gone by and set SKU-wise, Customer-Wise volume and value targets with the consensus of the frontline sales officers and sales representatives. I gave my talk as always and was witnessing the numbers being reviewed when it struck me that in today's world, planning for a month and quarter made people sell only in the last week of the month. That's when an idea flashed in my mind that every salesman should be given daily SKU-wise targets and one simple daily value secondary target. For those who are new to the FMCG business, Primary sales is the sales from a company/Super Stockist to the Distributor and Secondary sales is the sales from the distributor to wholesale/retail outlets. Salesmen visit shops in a route for one distributor or two distributors in a day and do secondary sales. So, when I discussed this move to a daily sales system, as usual there was resistance to change. Barring my ever-enthusiastic managers, the mood was sombre. I could feel the energy levels dip and during lunch, most of the front-line salesmen were talking amongst each other. I knew that they believed that this is an additional burden and impossible to do. After the lunch session I got my senior managers to explain how this system would actually reduce every salesman's stress. I too explained to the salesmen that doing and tracking one's own daily sales is like studying for a final exam everyday vis-à-vis cramming on the last day. This is how they had been approaching sales and running like headless chicken in the last 3-4 days of every month to achieve their month's targets.

*Refer to Appendix for report formats

* * * * *

Profits Aren't Everything, They Are the Only Thing for a Small Business

We live in a world of VC-funded startups and Shark-Tanks, where valuation is everything, and fund-raises at valuations that are astronomical make headlines! After all the shoo-sha, as has happened with many Indian unicorns already, when the company goes in for an IPO (if at all), the retail investor will end up sitting on big losses. While there are exceptions, unfortunately there have been too many startups that have played and continue to play this short-term game where living-together and pre-nups (for exits) are better than marriages for life. Honestly, as an old-timer, I do not understand this game and in many cases do not believe it is a very healthy one (There are always exceptions and I talk about this in the next Chapter – What I Think About Valuations). Venture Capitalists are very much needed to help the entrepreneurial ecosystem, and not for a minute do I discount that. But my focus is on entrepreneurs who wish to build profitable consumer-product brands and businesses that God-willing can be passed on to the next generation, and not those who wish to build and sell in 7 years to give VCs and themselves exits.

So, when you are running a bootstrapped startup or are the 2nd or 3rd generation owner of a family business, profits aren't everything, they are the only thing. In the traditional world of business value has to be created for all stakeholders.

How do we do this? Sound Unit Economics. What are unit economics? It means that there has to be sufficient gross margins for each product being sold. It means that the variable costs (costs that increase in proportion to number of units of a product sold) should be significantly less than the price at which the product is sold.

Today, in addition to the traditional channels of B2B2C (Business to Business to Consumer), we have B2C or the new buzzword D2C (Direct to Consumer). As per my experience, to run a profitable business, for traditional channels of B2B2C where the company sells to a Super Stockist/distributor and they in turn sell to retail/wholesale who in turn sell to the end customer / consumer, a normal healthy gross margin would be 20-40% on the sale price before tax (GST/VAT). This is for fast-moving consumer products with high volumes and low margins. For D2C a good ballpark we use is product landed cost (material cost plus inward freight & direct labour could be included for goods manufactured in a company's own factory) should not be more than 50% of the MRP. While there are different ways of doing product costing, that is not in the scope of this book, so I will not complicate things.

If we follow these ballpark gross margins, after all overheads the company is left with a decent net profit margin. Now what about the overheads? Every company has direct and indirect overheads. I refer to direct overheads as overheads or costs directly attributable to sales, like salaries of salesmen and sales teams. Other overheads include all other salaries, rents, electricity, statutory expenses, water, office consumables, outward freight (Though this is a variable cost, it is taken as a % of sale value because it varies depending on where the product is shipped to) etc.

So, in the consumer-products business we must sell volumes sufficient to cover the overheads and make a margin. So, if we have a gross margin of 50%, and we budget to sell $ 1 million of products, we must make a budget of overheads not exceeding 40% if we have to make a 10% net profit margin. So, the way to do it is to knock of the profit you want to make from Sales of $1 million (i.e., 10% of $1 million = $100,000), subtract the variable costs which are $ 500000 =>

$ 1 Million – $ 100000 (Required Net Profit) – $500000 (Variable costs/cost of goods sold) = $ 400000

So, your organization must aim to keep all overheads less than or equal to $ 400000 to be able to be profitable in that financial year.

* * * * *

How we changed a dangerous credit-based sales process to a 100% advance payment system overnight to achieve a negative working capital

The year was 2015, and I was glancing through the balance sheet and P&L of the previous year. Receivables (Amount due from customers) had steadily increased across all states. For a small business, if profits are everything, cashflow is oxygen. There is no point achieving great revenues and profits if the money is lying with Super Stockists and Distributors. In 2015 we were still primarily into stationery products and the stationery products industry is a severely credit-oriented industry. I was in a dilemma as to how to curtail this before it snowballed into a major cash-crunch for the organization. However, we had one case-study in Karnataka, where a very good manager by the name Krishna Deshpande had voluntarily done the unthinkable. He had converted the entire state's business to advance payments around 2013, though I am a little unsure of the date. While he had done it, our major market of TN and Kerala and AP were still hesitant to make the shift. One night I decided that we had to pull the trigger and called my regional managers Sakthivel and Balu and told them that I have decided to make the organization a 100% advance-based sales organization. There was silence from the other end, but both of them being phenomenal leaders, said they would back me to the hilt. As you would have read in an earlier chapter, Balu did so after a rightful fight and sleeping over it. We knew it was a big risk and had no idea by how much our sales would dip, and whether our distributors would move to our competitors. But a decision was made and from the next day, the necessary communications started going out that we would be giving 2% extra cash discounts, but all payments would be 100% in advance. This system was implemented barring two of our oldest and biggest customers in TN, as they had never delayed payments for over 4 decades – We gave them too credit only for ink sales and not for the rest of the stationery SKUs. Relationships also must be considered when big changes are made and that is exactly what we did. There were a lot of sighs of disbelief by the frontline salesmen, which was expected because they now had to complete all old dues collections and work the markets much harder to get primary sales from the distributors and Super Stockists. In most FMCG companies, when credit is involved, there is a lot of dumping of stock that happens at the Super-Stockist and Distributor points. This happens more for products that are slow moving and it creates a bad system of inflated primary sales, with delayed cashflows or at times NPAs (Non-Performing Assets or bad debts). The managers handled this transition extremely well and we told them not to worry about short term reduction in sales, but to follow the new playbook. Sales that year dipped by around 30% but barring a few miniscule bad debts we were now a 100% advance payment sales machinery in an otherwise credit-riddled industry!

This was huge for a small business because we were now a negative working capital organization, utilizing our capital much better. What is working capital?

Easily put, in an FMCG business it is:

Stock (Inventory) + Sundry Debtors (Receivables) – Sundry Creditors (Payables).

So, in an advance payment system, Sundry Debtors becomes 0 and we enjoy a 30-45 days credit cycle, as we take our supplier relationships and payments very seriously and ensure on-time payments. So normally Inventory-Sundry Creditors would be almost zero or slightly negative. This means we have very little to no capital blocked for operations and hence return of working capital employed becomes high.

Now for most startups and organizations, achieving negative working capital is not easy. So, what is acceptable working capital? In my experience for a product with gross margin 20%, going through the traditional distributor-wholesale/retail channels the working capital can be equal to the sales in a month.

So let us assume your company does INR 10 lakhs sales per month. Then the working capital Stock+Receivables-Payables can be Rs. 10 lakhs. So, for example, if your stocks at any given point is around Rs. 5 lakhs, your receivables are Rs. 10 lakhs and payables are Rs. 5 lakhs your working capital will be Rs. 10 lakhs (INR 1 million).

Now the whole game in the fast-moving consumer products business is the speed or velocity of turning around working capital, which companies like HUL, Marico, P&G, Godrej etc have mastered over the years.

What is working capital turnover ratio?

It is Sales per Annum/Working Capital. This ratio is also referred to as speed, because the more number of times working capital is turned over in a year, the higher the return on capital invested in current assets and overall ROCE also.

Now the formula for Return of Working Capital is nothing but

Sales per Annum/Working Capital X Gross Margin/100 X 100

Taking the same example of Rs. 1 million (Rs. 10 Lakhs) per Month and Working Capital of Rs. 10 lakhs at any given point, the return on working capital would be as follows:

⇨ Rs. 1,000,000/month X 12 months / Rs. 1,000,000 X 20/100 X 100

⇨ 12 (Speed) X 20 (gross margin)

⇨ 240%

Another way of looking at it is 20% gross margin on Rs. 1.2 crores (Rs. 12 million) annual sales = Rs. 2400000 (Rs. 2.4 million)

2400000/1000000 X 100 = 240%

Do you see how gross margin and speed impact return on working capital? This is what you should groom your sales teams to achieve to run a profitable small business. It's almost like a miracle that a small investment of Rs. 1 million (Rs. 10 Lakhs) turned around 12 times in a year with a product that has just 20% gross margin results in a whopping 240% return on working capital!

Another important aspect an entrepreneur in the consumer-products space must keep in mind is that the current ratio should be >1 i.e., **Cash+Receivables+Inventory/Current Liabilities (Payables) should be >1.** This means that the current liquid assets are sufficient to cover liabilities and party payments that are becoming due within 1 year.

* * * * *

What Should You Measure?

Parts of this chapter are an elaboration of the chapter: 'How We Moved from Quarterly to a Daily Sales Discipline and How You Can Too'. But I am repeating this here because it is very important to understand how it is done.

For many years, honestly, I would evaluate monthly sales, product-wise sales, customer-wise sales, production, and stock movement analysis at the SS/Distributor Point (Movement analysis is nothing but Opening Stock+Purchases-Closing Stock = Secondary Sales) for the month or quarter. Purchases are nothing but primary sales from company to SS/Distributor. The managers would review the daily sales reports (unit and value sales of each product from distributor to retail/wholesale outlets) filled by hand by each salesman, every month before approving travel and daily allowances. While this is what most business leaders do, sometime around 2012/13, I realized that the sales guys were not as productive as they could be. I felt that they did not have clarity of what they had to do daily. So, I called for a meeting with my managers and told them that I wanted to have daily targets prepared from the quarterly and monthly targets being set. This would be a simple value that every salesman had to achieve. This was a way to prevent billing only in the last week of the month and smoothen out primary sales to a near-daily occurrence. While I initially didn't have the buy-in from managers because they felt the salesmen might quit, I insisted that this would in fact help salesmen achieve their monthly and quarterly targets with less stress. As predicted by the managers, the initial days were tough and compliance levels were low as it is with any change and human beings. But we persevered and kept at it and also highlighted the salesmen who were profit centres and those who were cost centres on a daily basis. We did this by adding a column CTC/Sales in the DSR that the managers would fill and share with their teams daily. Daily CTC (Cost-to-Company) was calculated as A salesman's (Monthly Salary + Average Monthly Daily Allowance + Average monthly Travel Allowance)/30 Days. This way if the salesman had done sales such that his Daily CTC (Cost to Company: Salary + TA + DA)/Secondary sales done to wholesale/retail on a given day is less than 5% or 3% depending on the state of operation, he would know he is justifying his salary.

This exercise was to help the frontline sales guys understand their contribution to the organization, and those who achieved the quarterly targets are incentivised at 1% of the growth over the same period in the previous year.

Along with this daily value targets, each salesman had SKUwise target sheets that had the month's target, CMLY (Current Month Last Year) Sales, Daily Target, and Cumulative Target. Each day they would fill out their units achievement beside each SKU (Stock Keeping Unit) in the achievement column and then add today's achievement to the previous day's cumulative sales column to get cumulative sales up till date.

So, in effect, you plan for the quarter Customer-Wise, SKU-Wise for each salesman and get the total target in value terms and then divide this total value by the number of days in the quarter, to get a simple daily value target. This value target along-with the SKU-wise target sheet should be used daily by every salesman so he/she has data at his fingertips. We have largely automated this, but we see that making people write SKU-wise daily achievement produces better results.

*Refer to Appendix for report formats

* * * * *

OKRs and KPIs

While the daily targets, DSRs and product-wise target sheets had a significant impact, I felt the system could be further fine-tuned in line with our Nishkama Karma Value system where we measure efforts more than outcomes alone. So, in 2021, I read up about OKRs (Objectives and Key Results) that were implemented and popularized by Google. So, we broke down the OKRs, specifically for the sales team to the following daily must do objectives and key results:

- 60 calls per day (i.e., visit 60 stationery and FMCG outlets in a day).
- Ensure there are 20 productive calls at least.
- Get the contact details and call/visit 2 new distributors daily (To build our distributor database for the future)
- While doing this, they have to achieve their KPI or Key Performance Indicator of <5% or <3% CTC/Sales% depending on the State (territory) of operation.

In a nutshell, take every department in your organization and see how you can measure effort and set OKRs and then measure the KPIs. For example, for your brand team it could be number of contests or BTL activities carried out every month or quarter. It could be a measure of the consistency with which the brand is placed in front of the consumer.

It could be number of new marketing ideas generated (Using them or not is next. But the key is to think hard and deep about how to get intimate with your consumer and delight him/her. It could also be number of free samples sent out or distributed.

For Finance, it could be a measure of non-strategic costs reduced every quarter. There could be a clash between marketing and finance, so it's best to set marketing budgets and tell your finance team that this budget is sacrosanct. For production it could be number of units produced per day with wastage less than tolerance. While I am stating things we are experimenting with, you should make sure OKRs and KPIs of all departments work cohesively and produce desired results and growth for the organization.

*Refer to Appendix for report formats

* * * * *

Culture, Culture, Culture

My grandfather Dr. N. Jayaraman and my father Dr. J. Rajaram had done an absolutely awesome job of genuinely caring for every employee and their family. Being a small business, they could never pay very high salaries, but people stuck, because they felt cared for and felt like they were part of the family.

I am fortunate to inherit this Culture and continue to do whatever I can to help employees when they need it. Whether it is the birth of a child, an educational loan, extra leave for a medical emergency, all these are taken care of by my father, me, and our managers. So, this really is a family business at its heart and it's all about the intimate bonds that we share with every employee. Several employees and their children work with our organization, and this is awesome. When I read 'Predictably Irrational' by Dan Ariely, I realized that at Bril we could never afford market salaries and perks, but somehow my father and grandfather had kept loyalty super high. I learnt from my father and continued to emulate him the best I could. So why is it that employees stay with Bril and are so passionate about it? It is because of something Dan Ariely calls social norms. Social norms far outweigh market norms, till they are substituted by market norms. These days companies are trying to buy loyalty through higher salaries and perks, but it just doesn't seem to be working. Once companies move from social to market norms by hiring and firing in an inhuman manner, it is almost impossible to go back to social norms as per Dan Ariely's experiments, because trust is lost both ways. We see this happening in the biggest Tech companies that talk a lot about inclusiveness, equity and caring for their employees, but layoff inhumanly by locking people working from home, out of their systems with zero notice. In such cases, employees say, why the hell should I be loyal to any company? This is a natural human reaction, right? Let me give you an example. Go home today and pay your wife, husband, or mother for the amazing dinner they made. I am guessing you already know what their reaction would be right? You just breached a social norm of family doing things for one another for the love they share with each other. Similarly, imagine explicitly telling your girlfriend that she owes you one because you spent USD 500 on a good meal – best of luck with the relationship 😉! On the other hand, if you buy your mother or wife a nice gift, how will that make them feel? Appreciated right? Human beings operate in distinct social and market norms, while organizations should learn how to leverage social and market norms in humane ways. In the organizational context, when people feel they are cared for, they move to a social norm and work to fulfil the common mission. Am I saying pay less and use social norms? No, I am saying pay the best you can and then add all the soft elements of genuinely caring for and doing what's best to help employees when they or their families need the help.

For several years, till around 2020 when Covid struck we would all refer to the team as the Bril family. But in 2020 when all hell broke loose, many companies were laying off people because they didn't have business, it got me thinking.

By God's grace we didn't have to lay off anyone, and we put in our own funds to pay full salaries when sales were at 30% of normal years, for 2.5 years, because schools were closed! But what I questioned to myself at that point is that, is an organization your family? The introspection made me realize that there is a big flaw in this analogy, because no family sacks a family member and very rarely do family members abandon their family (even if they do, the blood relationship won't change in cases where there is a blood relationship). With the mass layoffs that are happening in the tech sector in 2023 as I write this, it is even more clear that this whole 'family ' culture is a farce. While we at Bril never let go of employees unless of course there is an ethics issue, attitude issue or consistent non-performance or values mismatch, I was seeing the biggest of organizations flush with funds letting go of great employees, for no fault of theirs. This made my conviction about setting right our culture immediately. While balancing the great aspects of our core culture that had leveraged social norms, without of course doing it intentionally, we needed to understand that we have come together as a team to achieve market outcomes. The next chapter talks about just this.....

* * * * *

Your team is not a Family it is an Army. Growth Mindset

So, during that phase of deep introspection, I wrote an email to all my employees stating that we would no longer refer to ourselves as the Bril Family. While nothing would change in the way we care for each other and our families, we will call ourselves the Bril Team or Bril Army. I explained to them that army personnel and their families genuinely care for each other and look out for each other, but there is never any room for non-performance or lack of ethics in an army. So, the message was to say we are an army with a common Vision, Mission and Value system and will be together till that alignment is there. When a person is not aligned to the organization's Vision, Mission, and Value System they are free to leave or in rare cases they are let go off.

What this change did was it reemphasized the importance of performance and growth, while firmly establishing the humane touch for all stakeholders of the business. After all our Mantra is To Make Living Fun!

When big tech companies that had referred to their employees as family and raised the pampering to multi-cuisine lunches, massage spas, play areas and free-flowing coffee, everyone was gung-ho. I wonder how the 'family members' felt when they were sacked with an email and locked out of their logins while working from home. Or had their IDs disabled and couldn't enter office even to say bye to their colleagues and collect their belongings. Isn't there a huge disconnect? Of course, there is. Neither should HR go overboard with a party environment in good times, nor should they be inhuman the way companies have been of late with huge layoffs especially in countries like the US and in the startup ecosystem in India. It's all about a very fine balance, and we all make mistakes at times, because we are after all just human. But, overall, we must stick to our core values, and they should be centred around the best we as an organization can do for all stakeholders, for a harmonious existence.

* * * * *

Recognize and Reward the Performers

For many years, when I was learning the ropes, sales managers would recommend equitable and low annual increments and target achievement incentives to those who achieved their targets. What this did was, it was demotivating the star performers as they were not getting very much more than the average and poor performers. This made good people leave. At this point we sat down and decided that we had to reward performers in a significant way and encourage them to grow. Performance was not limited to just revenues but also a person's attitude, proactiveness, achievement of OKRs and KPIs and relationship with his peers, seniors, and subordinates. This change made a big difference as it automatically got rid of the poor performers while bringing in a growth mindset in the team.

I don't know how true it is, but I recently read somewhere that there are some schools in the US that are not sharing the achievements of students, to prevent the non-achievers from feeling sad/demotivated. I was shocked to read this because, what this does is, it eventually brings down the whole class to the average/mean. In the name of equality and being equitable these schools are not nurturing real talent and accomplishments of students. Every student is unique and special, so why not recognize every student for what they are good at? If one student is good at sports, another at helping his friends and another at academics, recognize and motivate them to leverage and improve on their strengths, while working on their weaknesses.

So, in your organization, always make sure you and your leadership teams reward and recognize the performers. Do this using the right control systems and measurement metrics that work for your organization. So, intimate leadership is about tough love and taking tough decisions that are fair for the larger good of your people and your organization. Think of Intimate Leadership as the right parenting vs bringing up spoilt entitled children. So, decisions taken should be with the best interests of the organization and person/people concerned. If there is a chronic performance or ethics issue, letting go of that employee is best for the organization and the employee. Why for the employee? If the employee is unable to perform at all on this role, he/she will definitely find a better opportunity outside that suits their personality and skillset. If it was an ethics issue, it sends a message to all employees that ethics lapses will never be tolerated in the organization. The employee who has committed the ethics lapse will hopefully never do it again in the next organization they go to. So, in being an Intimate Leader, never try to be loved by all. It's impossible and detrimental to the health of your organization.

You must be wondering why I emphasize rewarding and recognizing good performers when our value-system (refer Bril's Value System) says do your duty with other people's benefits in mind without hankering after rewards and recognition. It is simple, it is the duty of the leaders to reward and recognize people, so the employees understand that if they carry out their duties and responsibilities and go above and beyond to Make Living Fun for customers and all stakeholders, they will be rewarded and recognized by the leadership as a by-product! See how it fits in? While this looks simple, it has taken my team and me years of questioning why we do what we do and how we can do our bit to get our organization ready for the next 100 years (Only possible with God's grace of-course) by building a world-class team that in-turn would make this 60-year-old brand relevant to consumers today and in future. Having said all this, entrepreneurship is a journey and a marathon and not a sprint.

So, whether you are the leader of a team in a big corporate entity, or the owner of a start-up or family-business, it is your duty to become an Intimate Leader and truly care for your employees. It is your duty to reward and recognize the performers and make them feel special, so they stay and do the same for their peers and subordinates. When this happens, the team as a whole will make the customer-experience world class, because they are unified and will strive to fulfil the Vision and Mission of the company while upholding the value system. While it all seems complicated, when you as the leader start introspecting about what emotional business you are in and truly engage and communicate this with your team and subsequently the customers at every touch point / moment of truth, you would be well on your way to building a very good, highly differentiated brand / brands and a truly world-class organization!

* * * * *

Enjoy the Journey and Simple Joys of Watching Your Employees Grow Personally, Professionally and Financially

The day I travelled with an employee who was flying for the first time, made me feel like a proud father. The day I hear of an employee building or buying his first house, I feel the joy and satisfaction that Bril has in some way contributed to this. I have felt the elation of an employee travelling abroad on work for the first time, the joy of my employees coming in with sweets celebrating their children's academic achievements. A simple act of giving an old car owned by the organization to a deserving manager was appreciated by him for years. I didn't think it was a big deal. But I realized very soon that it was a big deal for him. It was his first car! Just small gestures that don't pinch the pocket, done with the best interests of the person concerned go a long way.

Remember that every organization, big or small touches people in more ways than one. As a leader, we are human first. I enjoy being able to experience the positive impact Bril has on the lives of not only our customers and consumers but also on every employee. While we are no TATA, Apple, or Nike yet, we are Bril, and over decades, by God's grace, we have been able to help real human beings build a happy life, nurture families, and grow professionally and financially. I liberally give unsolicited advice and encourage my employees to start investing and build a cash-flowing asset base. I keep talking about the importance of starting small. I have gifted my book Just Invest and Become Insanely wealthy to employees and their kids who I feel would benefit. I have a passion for investing and I share this with my employees so they can grow financially.

* * * * *

Think Beyond the Metros and Recruit for Attitude

I studied in an international school in Bangalore all my life and then went to Madras University for my Engineering in Information Technology. After my engineering, I worked for a year with an IT company and then joined my family business before doing my MBA from a leading business school (Great Lakes Institute of Management) in Chennai. When I was in Bangalore in my international school bubble, barring my 2nd class train travel with my parents and the cultural grounding I got thanks to my grandmother and parents, I had no idea what the real Bharath was. It is only when I joined engineering was I exposed to people from all strata of society. While it was a cultural shock and I initially found it very difficult post my protected international school experience, this exposure is what got me rooted. What shocked me most in my very first year of engineering was the treatment of my chemistry-lab partner who was from a Tamil Medium School, by the professor. The poor guy couldn't follow instructions or communicate in the English language, but the professor would mock him and not explain things in Tamil. This would infuriate me, because colleges shouldn't take people from schools that taught only in local languages if they cannot be humane and inclusive. While I did my bit to translate, I was not very good at technical words and nuances in Tamil. So, I stood up for the poor guy and called out the professor and told him to explain things in Tamil. Experiences like these combined with taking local trains, buses and having friends from different socio-economic backgrounds really helped me when I eventually joined my family business.

At Bril, we recruit people for attitude and the ability to learn. For roles like finance, we look for degrees like BCom/MCom, but for sales and admin disciplines we even recruit people with no degrees. My head of finance Padma Nagarajan is the daughter of one of our senior most employee who is an admin manager Mr. Nagarajan (he is almost 90 and he just retired in 2023!). Padma, an MCom post-graduate has learnt on the job and is an extraordinary finance professional. Her attitude is phenomenal, and she learns every day and I too get to learn ton loads from her. I quote Mr. Nagarajan and Padma for their amazing contribution to our organization and unflinching loyalty and love for the brand. We are not the best paymasters in the country by any yardstick, but we have families working for the organization across generations and I thank God every day for blessing me with such good people who nurture this brand and till date keep it alive for the benefit of our consumers.

We do not require people to know English as long as they are good at their local language, to be able to thrive in their environment. My executive assistant Nagendra is an MA in Kannada Literature and had limited knowledge of English when he joined. He has learnt basic English over the years and is a real asset who is on the ball and keeps mine and my dad's life in order. An added benefit is that he can read all statutory documents that are in Kannada and help me and my father. My sales managers and production managers like Sakthi, Balu, Anandarouj, Prabhu, Jayaram, Pranesh (R&D), Raman and Gopal have all been recruited for their great attitude and dedication to our Vision, and they have all grown with the organization over years. Those who wish to learn or improve their English are encouraged to do so by the company and we even sponsor classes for those who show interest. We live in Bharath, and our beauty is that we are united culturally despite the amazing diversity. We have 22 official languages, 398 languages (387 living and 11 extinct languages) and 19500 dialects! * So why this fascination for English and the colonial hangover? Companies like Zoho and Zerodha have proven that recruiting locally and recruiting from the grassroots not only helps India, but can also build phenomenal, highly profitable national and multinational powerhouses.

At Bril, one of our major consumer segments over the years have been Government school children, and we recruit people who understand this consumer the best. It would be absurd if a person like me, sitting in a bubble in Bangalore, took unanimous decisions for consumers who I may not fully understand. However, my sales leaders and managers have grown from the grassroots and understand not only the trade customers but also our biggest consumers in Tier 2 and Tier 3 cities and towns and also in rural markets. This doesn't mean we ignore the Metros. We have a small presence which has a lot to improve, in all southern Metros through traditional distribution channels and pan-India direct-to-consumer, with our consumer products, without touching modern trade **(Read why we avoid modern trade channels in later chapters)**. Later in the Book you will also read about how we built India's most loved and largest-selling balance bike Brilrider, as a purely online D2C brand primarily addressing affluent SEC (Socio-Economic Classification) A Parents of 1–5-year-old children. So, in our own little way we cater to the Metros, Tier 1, Tier 2, and rural markets profitably, because of our employees and their daily insights. The reason most D2C brands in India are burning so much cash is because they wrongly calculate the TAM (Total Addressable Market). Founders sit in Bangalore, get funded and build products that invariably work for the affluent and upper middle-class urban consumer only. However, on paper they are chasing an illusory opportunity of the entire population of India. In my opinion, we must address both segments and in a cost-effective manner if we are to build a powerful, profitable brand in India. Some examples of Indian companies that have done it brilliantly and continue to do so are TATA Consumer Products (Brands Examples: TATA Tea, TATA Coffee, TATA Salt etc), Marico (Brand Examples: Parachute, Saffola etc), Dabur (Chyawanprash, Honey, Odomos etc), Jyothy Laboratories (Exo, Margo etc), Godrej Consumer Products (Good Knight, Cinthol, HIT etc), Bisleri, Bajaj Consumer Products (Bajaj Almond Drops, Bajaj Amla Hair Oil etc) and Emami. Among the MNCs of course we have HUL and P&G who have several brands for every segment. I have only given examples of FMCG companies and brands here, but we have great consumer products brands like Manyavar by Vedant fashions, Peter England, Van Heusen, Louis Phillipe etc by Aditya Birla Group in the apparels space. We also have new-age brands like Smoor which are helping Indian chocolates compete in taste and form with the best in the world. Not to forget brands like KC Das and Asha Sweets that have built raving fans for their Indian Sweets and Savouries. All these brands need not cater to the entire Indian population but cater to the segment they target beautifully and profitably. So, consumer products have a broad scope. I have covered as many consumer product categories as possible in the course of this book.

So, as a family-business heir, a corporate leader, or a start-up founder, go to the grassroots to do your study and address the huge opportunity that is Bharath, while also generating employment and opportunities by recruiting locally.

* * * * *

Making Meditation a Priority, Showing Up Every Day and Being Vulnerable

I have been a mantra meditator for years and I do my Sandhya Vandanam and Gayatri Japa twice a day. For many years during my college days, I had stopped doing it and I restarted it after I got married. Meditation has given me clarity, focus and a sense of peace. Despite being a meditator for so many years, the Covid lockdown and my mother being put on ventilator while all of us also were down with covid, made me an anxious wreck. To make things worse, Covid also took away my ability to sleep (I was a deep sleeper with no care in the world till I got Covid). The mind can be your best friend or worst enemy. I have experienced both ends of the spectrum of super clarity of thought, total peace of mind and heightened intuition and the darkest pangs of panic attacks and anxiety post covid. From the day I started seeing the benefits of meditation I have made it a point to encourage every employee in my organization to meditate and try to go to the no-thought zone at least for 10-20 minutes every day. I keep encouraging them to do this for their mental, emotional, and physical well-being and to experience how it greatly improves productivity and clarity of thought. While this is challenging, I keep at it during every meeting and during every interaction. Being a leader doesn't mean you have to be strong all the time.

During my worst phase, I showed my most vulnerable side to my employees. It got to a point where I couldn't go to my factory as I would get panic attacks. If I had tried to hide what I was going through, I would have never gotten the respect from my employees. My family and my entire team backed me up to the hilt during my toughest days. As an Intimate Leader, the more human we are the better we can connect with our people.

One thing is clear, anything that we touch and feel today was once just conceived as an idea or thought in the mind. So, visions come true when thoughts are converted into focussed, dedicated action and unflinching belief in the almighty or the universe or whatever you believe in. When I was going through my worst mental health battles, God showed me how much I had taken for granted. He showed me that the monkey-mind, if not controlled can become ones worst enemy. An idle mind is a devil's workshop came true during the covid times as business was down and there was negative news all around, but we still had to pay our employees. By God's grace we had the funds to do so. Despite my struggles, I never stopped sitting down with my eyes closed for 20-30 minutes in the morning and 15-20 minutes in the evening, though it was impossible to enter the no-thought zone and calm my mind during my battle with anxiety. Slowly, but surely over the last two years I am, with God's grace able to be in the moment again, albeit a huge distance from what I could achieve earlier. This is one of the most important aspects of intimate leadership because in the kind of uncertain world we live in with pandemics, layoffs, losing loved ones unexpectedly, wars and more, the only thing we must gain control of is our own mind. I urge you the reader, leader and human-being to take meditation and mindfulness seriously. If you are human, you need to care for your mind and reach frequencies that attract abundance and growth.

* * * * *

Say Sorry When You Are Wrong

Leaders who feel they are always right never garner any respect from their teams. We are all humans, and we all go through ups and downs in our lives and emotions. Sometimes, we could have had a bad day at home and take it out on our employees for no fault of theirs. Sometimes we could have made a mistake in understanding something or someone and called them out wrongly. As human beings there are a hundred different mistakes we can make despite the best of our intent. I have personally reprimanded someone wrongly and then publicly apologized for doing so, because I realized my mistake. Just a heartfelt apology and moving forward is something that we have made a part of our culture. We can have fights in meetings, but personal attacks are never tolerated. The fights, debates and arguments would be to come to an important decision to take the business forward. While debates are essential, once a decision by the leadership is taken, it must be followed through. The decision may be wrong and could be changed at a later date, but it is important for the entire team to give it their best effort and then decide on a different course of action if the decision taken didn't work. When this happens, leaders must take the blame for the wrong decision and move forward. Entrepreneurship is a humbling game and there is really no room for big egos.

* * * * *

Brilrider – India's First and Most Popular Balance Bike – How We Overcame Resistance to build a highly loved D2C Brand

When my son Raghav was born in 2010 is when I decided Bril would enter the Baby and Children's space. We launched three products - Brildiapers, Brilbooster (A Booster Chair) and Brilrider (A balance bike). Of the three, two failed and one succeeded. The Brilrider, a bicycle without pedals, trainer wheels or brakes that helps toddlers learn to balance a bicycle by the age of 2/3 years became a huge hit. Today Brilrider is India's most loved, highest-selling balance bike, but when we started off in 2011 it was not at an easy task. When we started as the first mover, we were creating a new category or even a new market in India. We had created a product that most consumers had no idea about the problem it would solve. We had designed and patented the product in India, but our traditional channels in the FMCG space could not reach the affluent parent who has travelled the world and would be an early adopter. We would ask our sales guys to do demos in parks and in beaches over weekends, but the feedback we got was 'why would we pay Rs. 3990 (price during launch) for a bike without pedals, brakes, or trainer wheels?' We tried placing the Brilrider in cycle shops and toy shops, but they were being returned in a few months. This was because consumers in India had to be educated about this product which they have never experienced before, and no shopkeeper could sell it convincingly. I soon realized that I could not use my salesmen or traditional retail to reach this completely new demographic. So, slowly we moved online in 2013 and started asking our few early-adopter customers to share videos of their little ones riding the Brilrider (This was well before D2C became a thing). We started sharing these videos on social media and ran some YouTube ads and that's when enquiries and sales on our website started picking up slowly. I have to thank my brother Raghunath, who is a designer for the beautiful packaging, logo design, branding and video edits for customer submitted videos of the Brilrider (These elements have played a major role in the Brilrider's aspirational appeal). The huge advantage with online ads was and is the ability to hyper target your customers. I handled and still handle the online and social media advertising myself. Brilrider's target audience was super well-defined – Parents of 0–3-year-olds in India with a household income > Rs. 4 lakhs per annum. This targeting to this day yields amazing results. We built the Brilrider brand completely using user-generated content and videos that we used to advertise online and on children's channels like NickJr. We ran share and win competitions on Facebook and gave away a free Brilrider to the person who shared and engaged the most with our videos. We ran these contest for several months and the buzz got louder and louder. With Instagram coming into the mix people started voluntarily tagging us with videos of their 2/3-year-old balancing the Brilrider. This was a wow product, and we leveraged the emotions of Fun/Joy (For Parents and the child), Excitement (For the parents to witness their 2-year-olds balancing a bicycle is a real wow moment which I personally experienced when my son first balanced his Brilrider), Love and Freedom (for the child who could zip on two wheels). This was it! We were not selling a balance bike, we were selling the emotions of Fun/ Joy, Excitement, Parental Love and Freedom. We distilled these emotions into a tag line 'Your Baby Can Balance with The Brilrider!'. All the videos we got from customers we added our logo, this line a jingle and a good VO. Cost-effective yet super effective, 100% user-generated content! So, this chapter shows us that Intimate Leadership is also about identifying and leveraging those intimate emotions that customers / consumers feel for their loved ones. When their child learns to balance the Brilrider, parents are so thrilled that they voluntarily write to us thanking us for such an amazing product. While they thank us for the product, we know what they are actually thanking us for is the shared emotions of joy, excitement, exhilaration, and love that they are able to share with their baby! This is also a case-study on the importance of user-generated content and ads. People blogged about the Brilrider, some became Bril Resellers and started promoting the Brilrider on YouTube Channels, Instagram, and their blogs, 100s participated in our video contests and shared videos of their kids balancing and riding their Brilriders. The Video contests were very successful because we select the best videos to advertise on television and create an additional wow for the parents, of seeing their child on national television! If we had to create these ads with models, it would have cost us several lakhs of rupees to just make the creatives and it would have less credibility among an informed consumer. So, at every stage the product, the experience, and the marketing Make Living Fun!

An Image of our Flagship Brilrider Flight AF Balance Bike

* * * * *

Pricing and Price Elasticity

'The single most important decision in evaluating a business is pricing power' – Warren Buffett

The big question for any entrepreneur is how to achieve pricing power or price inelasticity (or even better positive price elasticity). Basically, the brands that can increase price with little to no reduction in demand (or even better, an increase in demand) are the strongest brands.

So, what is price elasticity / inelasticity? Simply put,

$$\text{Price Elasticity of Demand} = \frac{\%\text{ Change in Demand}}{\%\text{ Change in Price}}$$

Or ((Q2-Q1)/Q1 X 100) / ((P2-P1)/P1X100)

Where

Q1 = Initial Quantity at Initial Price P1

Q2 = Quantity When Price is Changed to P2

Normally there is always an inverse relationship between price and quantity (i.e., if price increases, demand or quantity decreases and vice versa). This means Price Elasticity for most consumer products is negative because, if for example price is increased from Rs. 100 to Rs. 110 (i.e., +10% Price Change), Demand or Quantity would Change from say 1000 units to 800 units (800-1000/1000 X 100 = – 20%)

So, in the above case Price Elasticity would be (-20%)/10% = – 2. This essentially means that for every 1% change in price there is a 2% change in quantity, and they are inversely proportionate. So, for a 1% increase in price of the product there would be a 2% decrease in quantity and for a 1% decrease in price there would be a 2% increase in quantity.

In the same example if Price were to Reduce from Rs. 100 to Rs. 90, the Quantity or demand would go up from 1000 units to 1200 units so Price Elasticity Would be ((1200-1000)/1000X100)/(90-100)/100X100) = 20%/ (-10%) = – 2

Many economists and marketers remove the negative sign because they assume that price elasticity of demand is always inversely proportionate. But I like to look at it as follows, to be able to build **powerful Price-Inelastic brands – I.e., 'Marginally Elastic – Inverse Correlation', 'Marginally Elastic – Direct Positive Correlation' or 'Significantly Elastic – Direct Positive Correlation' Price brands.**

See Table Below to understand these terms:

Value	Elasticity	Meaning	Example
Infinity	Perfectly Elastic	When a small change in price of a product causes a major change in its demand, it is said to be perfectly elastic demand. In perfectly elastic demand, a small rise in price results in fall in demand to zero, while a small fall in price causes increase in demand to infinity.	Fiat currency for example would be perfectly elastic. If we charged Rs. 2 for a Rs. 1 note, demand would become zero. If we charged, Rs. 0.5 for a Rs. 1 note, demand would become infinite.
<-1	Significantly Elastic – Inverse Correlation	When a change in price occurs, a higher percentage change of demand occurs in the opposite direction. I.e., If Price Increases, Demand Reduces by a higher percentage and vice versa	Non-essential and essential goods that have substitutes. Most weak brands in the consumer-products space that compete on features, benefits and price come into this category.

>-1	Marginally Elastic – Inverse Correlation	When a Change in Price occurs, a lower percentage change in the demand occurs in the opposite direction. i.e., If Price increases, Demand reduces by a lower percentage and vice versa	Powerful FMCG and consumer brands fall into this category. Where price increase reduces volumes but at a lower percentage, hence achieving overall better profitability at the small cost of market share. Entrepreneurs and leaders can build very strong businesses even if they achieve this level of price elasticity for some of their products.
-1	Unitary Elasticity – Inverse Correlation	Percentage change in price results in same percentage change in demand in the opposite direction. e.g., If price increases by 10%, Demand Decreases by 10% and vice versa	Does not usually happen in real life. A theoretical example would be if there is a demand for 100 balls at Rs. 10 per ball, if the price increases by +10% to Rs. 11 per ball, the demand would reduce to 90 balls or – 10%
0	Perfectly Inelastic	Percentage change in price does not cause any change in demand	Doesn't happen in real life, but if the world were to run out of drinking water for example, people would be willing to pay any price for it, subject to affordability

<1	Marginally Elastic – Direct Positive Correlation	When a Change in Price occurs, a lower percentage change in the demand occurs in the same direction. i.e., If Price increases, Demand increases by a lower percentage and vice versa	Now we are getting into the realm of extremely strong consumer brands where people are willing to pay a premium and demand increases albeit at a lower rate than the increase in price. This is where brands have an emotional connect with their consumers. Though there are substitutes available the consumer chooses your brand. This should be the sweet spot entrepreneurs and leaders should be looking for while launching new products. This is also where select few FMCG brands owned by Unilever, P&G, Marico, TATA, Godrej etc would fall.
1	Unitary Elasticity – Direct Positive Correlation	Percentage change in price results in same percentage change in demand in the same direction. E.g., If price increases by 10%, Demand Increases by 10% and vice versa	Normally does not happen in real life

>1	Significantly Elastic – Direct Positive Correlation	When a change in price occurs, a higher percentage change of demand occurs in the same direction. I.e., If Price Increases, Demand increases by a higher percentage and vice versa	This is the realm of super-luxury brands where a higher price increases a consumer's desirability and hence demand amongst that segment of consumers who can afford the brand. Though many economists may disagree with me on this point, the value of luxury brands like Louis Vuitton (LVMH) speak otherwise. The parent company LVMH Louis Vuitton, Moët & Chandon and Hennessy that also owns the brands like Givenchy, Bulgari and Sephora has a Market cap as on the date of writing, of Euro 438.64 billion and stands 11th in the list of companies with highest market capitalization! It was the first European company to cross USD 500 Billion in Market Capitalization in April 2023*

Table 1

So, what does the above table tell you? Brands that are in the business of emotions command better pricing power and price inelasticity of demand or a positive proportionate elasticity of demand. So, Intimate Leadership is also about knowing our consumers intimately and creating that intimate emotional chord with them. This is easier said than done, but if not done, you are out of business when the next product with better features and benefits enters or an MNC prices you out of business.

While we cannot build super-brands in the **Marginally Elastic - Direct Positive Correlation category** overnight, we should be at peace knowing that even many of the top brands in the world fall into the category of **Marginally Elastic - Inverse Correlation (I.e., If Price is increased, Demand reduces, but at a lower percentage than the price increase)**. What does this mean?

Let us look at an example:

Let us say your company has built a reasonably good emotional chord/intimacy with consumers for a beauty product (let us say an all-natural shampoo).

Let us assume you sell the product at Rs. 100 and you sell 1000 units in a particular year.

If the cost to produce the product is Rs. 30, your Gross Margin is Rs. 70.

Now if you sell 1000 units you would make Rs. 70000 without taking into consideration overheads (Sales Rs. 100 x 1000 units - COGS Rs. 30 x 1000 units = Rs. 70000)

Let us say marketing and other overhead fixed costs are Rs. 50000.

You make a Profit Before Tax of Rs. 70000 – Rs. 50000 = Rs. 20000 or 20% of Sales, before tax

Now let us say you wish to increase the price for higher profitability, to Rs. 120 per bottle

Assuming the cost has increased by 10% to Rs. 33

If your brand falls in the **Marginally Elastic – Inverse Correlation (I.e., If Price is increased, Demand reduces, but at a lower percentage than the price increase)** category, for the 20% increase in price, demand would reduce by around 10%. So instead of 1000 units you would sell 900 bottles (units).

Let us assume Overheads remain the same at Rs. 50000.

Sales = Rs. 120/bottle x 900 bottles = Rs. 108000

COGS = Rs. 33/Bottle x 900 bottles = Rs. 29700

Overheads = Rs. 50000

Profit Before Tax: Rs. 108000-Rs. 29700 – Rs. 50000 = Rs. 28300 (26.2% of Sales)!

Your profit is Rs. 8300 (41.5%) higher than when you sold 1000 units and earned Rs. 20000 in profits, even though you are now selling just 900 units!

Just for theoretical understanding, if we have to make the same profit of (Rs. 70000 gross and Rs. 20000 PBT) as case 1 where 1000 units were sold for Rs. 100 each how many units do we need to sell at the new price and cost?

Now Gross margin per unit 120-33 = Rs. 87/unit

Units to sell to achieve Rs. 70,000 Gross Profit = Rs. 70000/ Rs. 87/unit = 805 units

So, if you sell 805 units you will get Rs. 70035 gross profit, and if you deduct Rs. 50000 overheads you will be left with Rs. 20035.

So, this says if your brand is in the Marginally Elastic - Inverse Correlation category of price elasticity, and variable cost increases by 10%, you will make a higher profit by increasing your price by 20% till volume doesn't dip below 805 units (I.e., 19.5% dip in volumes/demand). If variable cost per unit remains Rs. 30 and doesn't increase to Rs. 33, then gross margin per product unit sold would be Rs. 120-30 = Rs. 90. Then you would have to sell only 778 units (i.e., Rs. 70000/90) to make the same profit. This means you are making a higher profit if you increase the price by 20% and volume doesn't dip by more than 22.2%!

This is the power of pricing! So, you can imagine the kind of profits you would earn if you build a strong brand that connects emotionally with the consumer and falls in the Marginally Elastic – Direct Positive Correlation category (where your increase in price would also marginally increase volumes over time, because consumers seek out your brand vis-à-vis other options they may have).

I will leave you with an image of the top companies based on Market-Cap Globally:

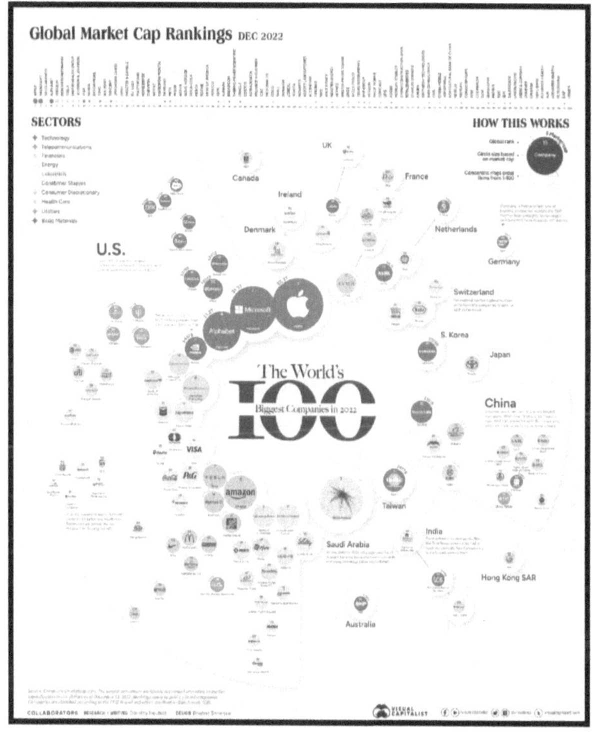

Source: https://www.visualcapitalist.com/biggest-public-companies-in-the-world-2022/

* * * * *

Why We Have So Far Avoided Modern Trade Channels Almost Completely

This is controversial and I do not recommend this to all brands, and I humbly accept that this maybe a wrong decision, which I could change in the future. Decide what works for you, but I share my personal experience here. When modern trade first emerged in India, we too got our products listed with a few chains. Soon we realized that it was more hype than real sales. While these modern trade outlets boast of great reach and footfalls, our experience and data tell us that the sales per outlet in modern trade is way lower than the average A class retail outlets or multi-brand smaller supermarkets in tier 2 cities. Despite knowing this after a year or two, we persisted thinking this trend would change and the future is modern retail only. As a couple of years rolled by, with marginal sales, some modern trade retailers started asking for heavy listing fees, obscene margins of 40% and more and returns of unsold inventory. This is when I started to get the feeling that being in modern trade was an ego trip like a front-page newspaper advertisement for low-value products. It wasn't making any sense from a business standpoint. So, we took the hard but necessary call to focus on what really works and stick to traditional retail, wholesale and direct to consumer through our website! Since we took this decision, we have only grown and not regretted it so far. Having said this, I do not rule out anything if market dynamics were to change. There is never a right or wrong in business, but just learnings and lessons.

* * * * *

Making the Fountain Pen Sexy Again, for The Environment and The Love of Writing

While the world is talking about AI/ML, generative AI, LLMs and ChatGPT, we at Bril seem to be going backwards! Or is it really backwards? It's for our future generations to say. Mindless consumption and plastic waste are ruining our environment and to see the impact our industry was having on the environment, we did a small study and came up with a mind-numbing result. Today, most school children use Ball-Point Pens, and most of them discard them when the refill runs out of ink. Our experience in the business shows us that an average 7th standard kid needs a minimum of 5 ball point pens to get through one school year. In order to be conservative and take into account less usage by younger children in lower classes, we conservatively assumed every child uses up and discards 2 plastic ball pens in an academic year. India has 15 Lakh schools, and we took the number of children at the lower end of the spectrum at 500 children per school. Can you guess how many plastic ball pens are going into landfill every year from schools in India alone?

15 lakh Schools X 500 children/school X 2 ball pens per year into landfill = 1.5 billion Pens Plastic Waste Generated per year from schools alone

Isn't this an obscene amount?

At Bril, pre-covid we ran a social media video contest, asking children to speak about this and send us videos and the results were great. Now we are taking this information to schools through letters and visits by our sales teams to encourage use of traditional fountain pens and fountain pen inks. We also conduct handwriting competitions as we have been doing so since my grandfather's time as fountain pens help improve hand-eye coordination and stability-flow balance. Fountain pens also improve handwriting to a large extent, which is a beautiful human art and a dying one in the age of computers. We discourage cartridge fountain pens unless the cartridges are refilled, because even cartridges are disposable plastic (However we still do manufacture cartridges and plastic bottles also, as our consumers find them convenient and as a brand, we are there to serve them). A good fountain pen lasts for years, and fountain pen ink from a glass bottle like Bril 60ml Ink significantly helps reduce plastic waste from our Industry. We have also entered the premium fountain pens category by supporting Indian hand-made and machine-made fountain pen manufacturers. So, do we stop selling ball point pens? No way. We never lose track of what the market demands and consumer-preferences as a for-profit organization. We are not activists and will go out of business if we sell only fountain pens and fountain pen inks in glass bottles. So, it is very important to note that a brand can communicate what's good for the consumers and the environment and do its bit to make the world a better place, but we should know where to draw the line and always keep the consumers-preferences and financial health of the business in mind. The world is an imperfect place, and we can do our bit in making it better, but we must survive first if we have to make any kind of impact. A brand's job is not to become a moral science teacher, but to fit right into the lives of consumers and solve their needs/problems when they need it the most. So, if a customer needs a Rs. 5 ball point pen to quickly sign a document on the move, should we preach to him about the benefits of using fountain pens and how he is destroying the environment with a ball point pen? No way! Never talk down to a customer – Branding 101. This is the subtle line that brands need to draw between activism or purpose or whatever the latest buzzword is and solving consumer-needs profitably. Rule of thumb: Consumer brands are inclusive by nature and can be used by anyone. So, unless you are targeting a very niche segment of consumers, an activist approach may jeopardize a large portion of your existing consumer-base and adversely affect your brand. Many marketers world-over seem to be forgetting this while they launch products and campaigns catering to one small segment of their existing customer base and antagonizing a major portion of their loyal customer-base. This is because, nobody likes to be told that they are bad. Powerful brands aren't built by making consumers feel small and bad about how they live their lives, but by making them feel special and being at their service no matter their religion, caste, creed, race, sex, orientation, or worldviews. While there are many examples in the recent past where even top companies have crossed this Lakshman Rekha, it is not in the scope of this book to give these examples, as I do not wish to delve on mistakes and negatives of any company. I merely wish to educate leaders about how, in my opinion and limited experience believe intimate leadership should work. In a nutshell, it is our duty as leaders, to enhance the lives of our employees, customers, consumers, shareholders, and all stakeholders.

As long as we do business in the most ethical way within the laws of the land we operate in and work towards minimizing the impact on the environment and Make Living Fun™ for all stakeholders, we believe we are true to our mission every day at Bril.

Puja for our brand new fully automatic cartridge assembly machine

* * * * *

Customer Delight is More Important Than Transactional Profit

You must be wondering how I say this, when I said profits are the only thing for a business? Read on...

A bright summer morning we got a frantic call from a mother who had just placed an order for a Brilrider Flight AF (Our top of the line, Airplane grade Aluminium, Ultra-Light 1.9 KGs, Sand-Blasted Anodized Metal Frame Flagship Model) on our website www.brilindia.com. For the mother, the model didn't matter, the price she had paid didn't matter, but something was troubling her. Her baby was turning 2 the next day and she had ordered the gift – The Brilrider Flight AF very late due to her work commitments. Now she wanted to know how long the bike would take to reach her. She lived in Bangalore and normally the courier would deliver the next day, but sometimes it takes 2 days. Without thinking, our manager in Chennai who took her call at the time, who unfortunately passed away in 2023, put the customer at ease telling her that the bike will be delivered by the same evening. He called the sales manager Anandarouj in Bangalore and asked him to drop everything else and head to our factory in Peenya, collect a bike and get it delivered to the customer at the earliest. The bike was delivered to the customer within an hour, and she was ecstatic. The entire team was gung-ho and I personally recognized Rajagopal, Anandarouj and all involved for this customer-centricity.

In the above case, we were lucky to also make a transactional profit, while delighting the customer and Make Living Fun for her and her family. But another example was of an elderly gentleman from Trichy in Tamil Nadu who had purchased a Rs. 15 Bril fountain pen and wasn't satisfied with the quality. When Sakthi our RSM received this email, he immediately swung into action and got the salesman in Trichy to collect 2 of our best fountain pen models (Worth Rs. 100) from our distributor there to hand over to the customer and take back the piece he was not satisfied with, for testing. This made zero financial sense from a transactional perspective but made 100% sense from a CLV (Customer Lifetime Value) perspective! The gentleman was so thrilled that he messaged us saying he was a teacher and had recommended Bril to all his students! These are just two of the many many adventures our teams have undertaken to delight even the smallest (in value terms) of customers, because the value of the transaction doesn't matter when it comes to our duty and Value System of Nishkama Karma. I hope you see how an intimate emotional bond is being built between the brand and the consumer each time there is a service recovery or doing the unexpected To Make Living Fun™!

So, for those entrepreneurs who are in it for the long haul, these interactions far outweigh blowing millions of dollars on advertising. A powerful brand is built one day at a time, one interaction at a time, over years, decades, and centuries. Again, do you see the role of human relationships and the core of Intimate Leadership? Do you see that every team member gets to be an Intimate Leader at some point or the other? It is our duty as leaders to set these priorities for our employees, so they know that they are empowered to take discretionary action to satisfy the customer without long approval processes. If in doubt, they should be able to pick up the phone and call their immediate manager of even you the founder/CEO and sign off immediately.

* * * * *

Investing your Profits in Assets for Future Growth Capital

When you are building a company that can hopefully stand the test of time, with minimal debt and no external equity capital, it is very important to create assets that your company owns. When you have sufficient profits and cash, majority of it should be reinvested into the company for compounding and growth, but a small portion should be invested in tangible assets like land. Sam Walton of Walmart would buy double the land needed for each store and sell the other half for a profit or hold it for many years to come. As of 2017 Walmart's real estate portfolio was said to be worth USD 230 Billion! We are a very small business comparatively, but at Bril, my grandfather and father would invest a small portion of the profits in land in their personal names or the firm's name. I have continued to do this, and this helps us take working capital loans or sell the land for fresh capital infusion when we need it to grow the business. Of course, FDs were taken regularly to keep unused capital earning some interest. While we haven't done it yet, I would also recommend looking at Bonds and Blue-Chip Stocks that are consistent compounders to park a portion of your cash in the bank in. As long as you don't invest more than 50% of your assets in financial instruments like stocks and bonds and they don't generate more than 50% of your company's income you will not need to register as an NBFC (Non-Banking Financial Corporation). All these investments are to help you build an asset base that you could use for future growth of your business.

* * * * *

Using Debt for Working Capital and Capital Expenditure

Debt is a very powerful financing option for businesses that have good unit economics and cash-flows to service repayments. As mentioned in the previous chapter, building an asset portfolio will help you use some of the assets as collateral to raise debt in the form of an overdraft or a term loan for capital expenditure and expansion. So, if you see, the asset base you build from your profits start helping in financing your future business growth without having to sell the assets. What this does is that it also minimizes risk as you are using your organization's investment assets to raise debt and not your personal assets. Entrepreneurship can be really hard financially for the entrepreneur and his/her family, as it requires huge sacrifices especially in the initial stages. While one may not have assets in the beginning of their entrepreneurial journey, one should always be aware of their family's needs before pledging personal properties like your house to fund the business. So anytime you consider taking debt be 100% sure that you have great gross margins and market acceptance to service the debt. You should have at least a 3-5 times interest coverage ratio (EBITDA/Annual Interest) to even consider debt as a safe financing option. I would strongly recommend only equity financing for newly born startups, if you don't have other personal or family investment assets that you can pledge and afford to lose in case your business fails.

* * * * *

We Pulled Our Products Out of Amazon

Most people thought I was crazy for doing this, but Amazon drove my team and me mad. We couldn't sleep. The Amazon ratings became everything for us, and we had to do anything and everything, including working some Sundays (to avoid getting a delayed shipment performance warning), to prevent someone from giving us a bad rating. It was crazy because, Amazon sadly doesn't take care of misuse of their customer-first policy when customers who buy at a whim, use the product, and return it. Even though the Brilirider (Which is the only product we listed on Amazon) came under the replacement only category, customers would ask for a refund. We would literally be forced into repaying the customer, to prevent the customer from giving us a bad review, as Amazon's whole consumer-centricity has put sellers (their first customers) under the bus. At one point Amazon started auto-approving refunds and we had to spend hours getting the call centre to deactivate that feature which they claimed was a part of the superior Easy Ship or something category they had 'upgraded' us to! At every opportunity they would give us these problems to nudge us to go for the Fulfilment by Amazon option which we didn't want to do for purposes of unit economics, and end-to-end control of the customer experience. We and most small business sellers are too small to try and change Amazon

(It's just not worth losing our sleep over it). Here we were, having the best product in the category, but having 20% returns on Amazon and just 0.5% returns on our website! Crazy right? We are already a customer-obsessed team, and we take replacements and refunds very seriously to ensure no customer ever feels short-changed, but Amazon took their 'policies' to a point where we decided that we no longer wanted to be on the platform and pay them 10% of our sale price and lose money on returns. We were doing the advertising and brand-building, so our sales dipped only by around 10% when we pulled out of Amazon (That's what we were paying Amazon anyway!). Further, we never listed our stationery and Home Care products on Amazon (At least as of writing this book) because what we found was that logistics costs for low-value products do not justify individual product orders. With Amazon, if we ever do list our lower value FMCG products, we will be selling only products that can be bundled to be more than Rs. 1000 to offer free shipping, as we also have to pay Amazon's commission in addition to shipping charges. On our website customers buy a combination of products to get their cart value to Rs. 750 to get free shipping. Now we are seriously evaluating ONDC to gain more visibility of all our products at significantly lower commissions (This could be a game-changer for many brands). I am not asking you to pull out of Amazon, Flipkart, or any of the marketplaces, but always do the cost-benefit analysis before succumbing to FOMO. Ask yourself whether it makes sense for your business and your team's wellbeing before following the herd.

Having said all this, when we first started off, we had to be on Amazon and Flipkart in addition to our own website, because visibility is everything when you are building a new brand. As Al Reis says in his 22 Immutable Laws of Marketing, what is most visible sells more than what is the best (and who is to say which product is the absolute best if it never sells?). Over and above visibility, Amazon gave the Brilrider the much-needed social validation in terms of reviews, as we were creating a whole new market category in India. We had a phenomenal 4.7 stars and 4.5 stars rating respectively for Brilrider and Brilrider AF for the 5 years we were on Amazon and Flipkart, and that created a brand worthy of going purely direct to consumer through our own website only. Amongst the new-age brands companies like bOAt have used Amazon beautifully to build a solid, profitable business. So never forget that to build and sustain good brand visibility, availability on various channels and platforms is very important. As entrepreneurs we must pick and choose what is right for our products/brand and what is not. The most important thing to note for all FMCG companies also, is that the future is tech and omni-channel. If brands stick to purely offline modes, it's going to be a herculean task to compete with the new boys and girls in town. In tomorrow's world it will all be about maximum visibility and who controls which ecosystem. Ecosystems are becoming moats for brands, and this is where the big boys are losing ground to nimble startups.

* * * * *

Future-Proof Your Business. Distributor Database Collection became part of Daily OKRs

Leads and a constant flow of leads is the lifeblood for any salesman, sales team, and organization. What we realized was, most of our salesmen just weren't planning for future eventualities of a distributor closing his business or switching brands. Most of our salesmen couldn't push distributors to supply to shops the distributor didn't want to supply to, or buy products they didn't see value in, for fear of losing the distributor. When we identified this problem, we decided that as a part of the daily OKRs every salesman had to get the lead of one FMCG distributor and one Stationery distributor in his territory, every single day. They had to do this whether they needed to appoint a distributor or not. This data till date gets aggregated and stored in our database and also goes into our email marketing autoresponder, so the leads are nurtured. The salesmen are asked to tell the distributors that they are collecting data so they could contact them if an opportunity and opening were to arise in their area. What this does is, it removes the desperation of having to appoint a new distributor after there is a problem with an existing distributor. It also creates the perception in the minds of the prospective distributor that there are no opportunities currently and makes them eager to join Bril when the opportunity (if at all) arises. So, this is a subtle way of creating demand in the trade channel.

* * * * *

Don't Advertise for the Sake of Advertising – Go BTL and Touch Consumers' Lives

You know, this is a topic which is very subjective, and I have covered parts of it in a small way in the chapter **'So How Do You Build a Powerful Brand?'**. But in the world of clutter, getting the attention of the customer when he has a need for the product you sell, your brand should be at the top of his mind. Large companies use huge ad budgets to achieve this, and there is no doubt that visibility, pulsing, and reach is everything when it comes to FMCG products. This category is essentially a volume game and the higher the share of mind of a greater number of people, more success will your brand have. This of course depends on your product solving the customer's problem reliably and effectively, repeatedly over long periods of time. So, this makes super-brands which become a part of the consumers' collective consciousness. However, if you are a small business or startup, believe me, you just cannot build a brand by trying to out-shout the big brands.

So, what we do at Bril is visibility on retail shelves in our core tier 2 and 3 markets, through good relationships with our distribution channels, lots of below the line promotions in schools and online engagement and advertising for D2C brands like Brilrider and catchy jingle-based fun regional language ads for FMCG products. For years we have had book labels and handwriting competitions to promote good handwriting. This directly has made Bril Ink a top-of-mind recall brand and product among school-going children and their parents, especially in schools in Tamil Nadu where fountain pens are still compulsory, primarily in Government schools. We regularly communicate the direct correlation between use of traditional fountain pens to improved stability-flow balance and hence better handwriting in children. Fountain pens and ink from a glass bottle are much more eco-friendly than ball-point pens, while also being easier on children's hands. So, this too is communicated to school managements and children through letters and our sales teams regularly. In addition to this, there is automatically an element of nostalgia that parents of school-going children have for Bril Ink as they associate it with love for their friends and the good times they had splashing ink on each other during their school days. The last emotional aspect is much stronger than the other logical and rational reasons to use Bril Ink. Please refer to the Chapter **'So How Do You Build a Powerful Brand?'**. The effect of nostalgia for people's school days and their association of these fun days with the Bril brand really amazes me. I was moved to see what my grandfather and father had built painstakingly over the years. A brand getting this much love is extremely rare and I thank God for the opportunity to build on this equity. Honestly, I don't even know if I have done justice to it so far! What is more amazing is that the brand Bril is a short-form of Brilliant, and this was coined way back in 1964 by senior-artist Late Gopulu. A brand like Bril is versatile because it can be extended across consumer product categories and still make sense, while it can also be used very effectively as the prefix or suffix to create more powerful brands (E.g., Brilrider, Brilours etc). So, this comes to the importance of creating brand names that stand the test of time. Brand names should be easy to pronounce and one to two syllables only.

The mistake a lot of new brands make is trying to advertise a lot with very poor distribution. Product availability through strong distribution is crucial before any advertising happens. Make product sampling and trials a part of your initial marketing mix and do it regularly through as many touch points as possible. Then move to the best possible below the line promotions like in-shop offers, contests, activations through radio channel partnerships, online contests, user-generated content, content marketing through informative blogs that inform your consumers on topics they care about, email marketing and PPC/ CPM social media and search engine marketing. The key is to induce trials and then through phenomenal product experience make consumers buy your brand again and again. For this to happen, there are a lot more elements to brand building than just pure-play mass media advertising. Building brands is an art and getting a permanent share in the consumer's mind is no easy task. Most marketers get lazy and splurge on advertising before their distribution is taken care of. What is the point in advertising when the product is not available on shelves? For D2C brands, though the availability is normally online, my experience says for most FMCG brands an omni-channel approach of online and traditional distribution is what ensures a larger market and better long-term profitability in a country like India. While I say go BTL (Below the Line), we do use television judiciously to generate long term equity and this too is important. We have used more television in addition to online advertising for our D2C product Brilrider. Brand-building as stated earlier is a marathon and continuous process and we must use every available channel effectively. I feel we should have used a lot more TV when there were fewer channels and no OTT. This is a mistake, but there is zero use crying over what we didn't do in the past. We have however made up for this by greatly leveraging the online medium since its inception.

Another innovative BTL promotion channel we have used very effectively is our Bril Ink Carton real estate. We have one panel dedicated to all our stationery products and more recently one panel dedicated to our new range of Home Care products. We realized that the parents of the students who use Bril Inks are our consumers for Home Care products and this ink carton sits in close to 60 lakh households for the entire year, year after year. A front-page newspaper ad is gone in a few hours to a day, a television ad is gone in 10-20 seconds, but real estate that sits on your consumers table or in a shelf in a consumers home the entire year is priceless. This is also real estate that the consumer looks at every time he/she must fill their fountain pens with ink! So, if you have a fast-moving product and have real estate on it, use it to promote your next product or new category if you will be servicing the same consumer or another consumer in that household.

Today, WhatsApp is becoming a great medium to share product updates with existing customers and many brands are using it beautifully. We are in the process of evaluating the best means of use of this channel to stay in touch with our existing customer base and new leads.

* * * * *

Allow Customers to Reach Real Decision Makers When They Have a Problem

Most big companies resort to call centres, which more often than not solve problems. The issue is when a customer has a problem that a low-level, inexperienced call centre employee is unable to solve. It gets really hard to reach a decision maker who can actually solve your problem quickly. I am sure most of us have at some point in our lives been frustrated with looping FAQs, IVRS and lack of a senior person to speak to who can solve our problem, while dealing with big companies. I have literally come back to this chapter to add a miserable experience my wife and I have been having with Airtel. I have been a customer of Airtel since 1998 and am supposedly a platinum or premium customer or whatever lip service term they use. My wife's number comes under my number in a family pack. We had recently taken two international roaming packs for both numbers while traveling to the US. We both had 100 minutes of incoming and outgoing calls free per day each, as a part of the packs which were taken for 30 days duration. We travelled only for 2 weeks out of the 4 weeks we had the packs for. So, we were charged for the 2 30 days packs upon our return. Till now it is fine. The subsequent month and billing cycle we got a bill for Rs. 3200 for outgoing calls to US numbers. While the amount is not significant, I knew there was a mistake immediately, as neither of us had exceeded the 100 minutes per day free calls and these charges were for the last week we were in the US. My wife and I independently tried reaching the call centre and it kept taking us in loops on IVRS as there was some input bug. So, we both registered complaints using the Airtel app. We waited for 2 days and neither of us got the promised call back. The bill date had passed by then and we didn't want our lines to get cut, so we desperately tried reaching Airtel through the call centre and App to no avail. After another couple of days passed, I went to the Airtel outlet. There the lady helped me reach the customer care. I explained to the customer care that the detailed bill statement clearly had only 107 minutes of outgoing and incoming calls for the entire duration of our trip on my wife's number which had the incorrect charges despite having one of the two international packs active. I explained that there was no way her number could have exceeded the 100 minutes free on any given day as the bills clearly showed the data of 107 minutes only across all days and no day exceeding 10-15 minutes of incoming and outgoing calls! The man refused to accept and said my wife's number had exceeded 100 minutes on 2 days during our stay, like a stuck tape recorder without being able to tell me why it was not reflecting as such in the itemised detailed bill in front of both of us. I spent an hour trying to explain simple maths to the guy who refused to escalate to a manager. He said I would get a call within 24 hours from the billing team. The call never came. My wife called the call centre again the next day and she had to repeat the entire story once again and wasted another hour to no avail. To make matters worse when she vocalized her displeasure when they refused to escalate, the man had the audacity to say she used profanities. The word she used was 'rubbish'. I wonder in which dictionary that is a profanity (She even has recorded proof of the calls). Basically, the customer was being bullied for a blunder by the company. Again, they said a call will come from the billing team and it didn't. The next day my wife called again and still the agent was unable to acknowledge a basic billing mistake and had no authority to escalate. My wife was on speaker and when she asked to be connected to a manager, we both heard the manager dismissing the agent saying the bill is correct (In Kannada), without even bothering to understand the case or speak to my wife. As I type this, I have paid the bill to prevent a disconnection and we got a call to an email we sent stating we had recorded all the calls, and we are being made to run around for a fault of the company. We have no idea if the amount charged will be rolled back. Even if it is, Airtel has completely lost the trust of one of its oldest, most loyal customers. The point is companies can hugely differentiate themselves by making senior decision makers available as soon as a customer problem cannot be resolved by the call centre. If managers hide and avoid facing customer problems and solving them, slowly but surely the business will lose, and the brand will get adversely affected. Is this an isolated case? Sadly, it is not. Most of us would have encountered the FAQs maze or the incompetent call centre with one big organization or the other. In fact, I have had some of the worst customer service experiences with dominant tech companies like Google and Facebook. They have phenomenal products, but in the rare occasion you need customer service or help, God save you. They do everything possible to make sure you can't speak with a real person. God knows what AI is going to do – when we desperately need a smart leader and decision maker to solve a pressing problem! I must say of the lot Microsoft has the best chat support (with real people), but recently I had a very bad experience with Microsoft too. OneDrive sync deleted all the files on my system. The chat support, though friendly asked me to make some changes which deleted my files from the cloud too! I mailed a dear friend of mine who is pretty senior at Microsoft, and he kindly mailed the OneDrive leadership. What happened? They went in loops, and nobody took ownership to call me to find out what happened. Bureaucracy and big-company-syndrome.at its worst. Imagine the plight of a person making a medical insurance claim not being able to speak with a decision maker when his/her big medical bill is not getting reimbursed? While on the topic, American Express sold me their most expensive charge card that costs Rs. 60000 per year. I reluctantly took it to see if it would help me with good travel benefits. Two months after I got the card which supposedly had 'no limits', my mother was hospitalized with Covid and spent a month on Ventilator. I too was down with Covid and had to go to the hospital as I was recovering as nobody else could. While we all had insurance and by God's grace sufficient funds, I tried to swipe my charge card for a Rs. 10 lakhs interim payment at the hospital. Guess what? It got rejected. I called the call centre and they apologized and said it needed special approval. I said I am trying to make a payment in a hospital, and it wasn't like I was buying a car! Nope, couldn't be done. I paid with my debit card and the very next day called to tell Amex not to renew this and downgrade me to the regular travel platinum card I had earlier, with an annual fee of Rs. 5000. A year went by, and I got a call from a sales guy in Amex to sell me the Platinum Charge card again. Wow! I told him that, I hadn't received a single call apologizing for rejecting the payment at the hospital despite me having no outstanding and a perfect payment track record for more than 10 years with Amex. He profusely apologized and then started talking about the perks the card offered. What's the use of perks when the core product failed me in an emergency? Why would any customer pay Rs. 60000 annually when the basic promise of no preset credit limit not being authorized/honoured even for an emergency? While they do rightly have terms and conditions and their system blocks high value transactions, no human being in the system had the authority to serve a loyal customer who was only trying to pay a hospital bill!

Now that I have shared the implications of poor customer service, let me share with you an amazing service recovery at Oberoi Cecil, Shimla during my family holiday there. There was a small mistake with the food delivered to our room. They had gotten the order wrong. We just mentioned it to the waiter who delivered the food and said it doesn't matter because we could have that starter instead of the one we had ordered. We finished our meal, and we received a call from the Chef. He profusely apologised for the mistake, and we told him that the food was excellent, and he really needn't apologize. The next thing we knew our room bell rang and guess what. The Chef had sent us a whole tray of the most unbelievable desserts, free of cost to make up for the very minor mistake. This blew our minds, as we had experienced some amazing service recovery and waiving the charge for the wrong item etc, this was a treat we will never forget. This is a classic way of taking a brand to stratospheric heights in the customer's minds. Similarly, Courtyard by Marriott Kochi Airport is a hotel I frequent. When they first started, their team was one of the best I had seen across hotels in India and world-over. Once when I travelled with my parents, wife, and son for a pilgrimage, we spent 2 nights at Courtyard by Marriott Kochi Airport. My son was around 4 years old then. The way the team at the restaurant took care of him and pampered him has to be experienced. He got free ice creams, pastries anything. He would ask and he would receive and not a single one of them was charged. We are parents who allow our kids to enjoy desserts in moderation and let them go berserk at times when on holiday. All of us just loved the hospitality and service and we still talk about it fondly. Believe me, we Indians and Asians have the best service levels in the world. Though the Hiltons and Marriotts of the world are American brands, the quality of service in their properties in the US and Europe are like a 3-star hotel or worse when compared to their service excellence in India and Asia. This excellence of service stems from our philosophy of 'Athithi Devo Bhava' (Guest is God) and the training many of their employees have had over the years with great Indian brands like Tak and Oberoi. Why am I talking about hospitality in a consumer-products book? Because these examples are to demonstrate the importance of customer intimacy and why we should all build organizations that are nimble enough to take 'out of policy' discretionary decisions within boundaries to help customers who have a problem or have had a bad experience. We should learn from the best 5-star hotels on how to handle service recovery, because no matter what business we are in, we are in the hospitality business and the moment of truth matters the most for each customer.

Building a business that has intimate leadership at its core means allowing customers to reach real decision makers when they need help or when they have a problem with the product or service. The huge differentiator that your startup or small-business can have over larger competitors is offering personalized customer-service by decision-makers. Even larger businesses should have a quick escalation mechanism to prevent poor customer-experience. At Bril, we have managers handling customer queries and issues. Customers love this because our leaders are empowered to take discretionary decisions to ensure customer-delight. Intimate Leadership principles like this can be adopted even by larger organizations by enabling quick escalation to mangers by call-centres when a customer is unhappy with solutions offered by lower-level employees. Unfortunately, many decision-makers and managers hide behind the call centre / customer-support teams and leave customers going around in circles when they really need help. As an up-and-coming startup or consumer-products brand, you as the leader can differentiate majorly by making decision makers interact with customers directly when they have a pressing problem. Quick resolution of problems sets apart great companies from the merely good ones. For example, when I had a problem with Zerodha, I mailed Nithin Kamath, the founder directly. Within minutes I got a response though we had never interacted before. He connected me with the decision maker in his team and I had the report I needed within an hour! Isn't that a wow? I will never forget this. Similarly, I try to reply to any customer who emails me and do my best to solve his/her problems. This culture also trickles down and my leaders and team members now know how important it is to prioritize customer problems and how service recovery greatly builds our brand. So, there have been several instances where my teams have gone above and beyond to satisfy customers as stated in the chapter **'Customer Delight is More Important Than Transactional Profit'.**

* * * * *

Kaizen in Product Development and R&D

Most Japanese companies do not communicate product quality in their marketing. But for years, Japanese products have had the highest scores on product quality amongst consumers. Communicating product quality when the product doesn't deliver on the promise when the consumer interacts with it, leads to an immediate disconnect. Most start-up founders and small-business owners tend to talk a lot about product quality in their marketing. What's really important is that the consumer makes up his own mind about the product's quality after using it. Nothing beats direct experience by a customer and word-of-mouth to communicate the efficacy and quality of a product. Whether it is through social validation like reviews or one customer talking to their friends and relatives about your brand, there is nothing that beats real consumer experience with your brand. As a brand manager / leader, our job is to ensure trials of our product by as many people as possible and then allow the consumer to become your biggest cheerleader. Think Apple. Why does the brand have so many vocal fans who fight for the brand? Does Apple say my product is of better quality than its competitor? No. Apple focuses doggedly on improving its products for superior user experience, right from its simplistic product design to UI to its seamless ecosystem. Similarly, if we look at Unilever's brand portfolio, they have some of the best products for personal care, home care and beyond, but seldom speak about quality. The company's duty is to continuously improve product quality while the products solve consumer problems better and better and make them love the experience more each time. This is to be done while marketing talks about the emotional needs the brand fulfils, to build strong, long-lasting intimate relationships with millions of consumers. Another example to note would be Gillette. Gillette has been improving their razors to super-smooth Mach 3 and Fusion 5 razors which have 3 blades and 5 blades. However, Gillette communicates self-love and aspirational value with 'The Best a Man Can Get' in all its communications and advertising and as a side note talks about its superior products. So, the combination of emotional connect with great products has helped it command ROCE of over 40% over decades.

At Bril, we have touched Over 480 million consumers over the years and continue to delight customers daily through our world-class products and great service. While we have faced several challenges over the years, what has kept us going is our single-minded focus on great consumer products that Make Living Fun for our consumers.

* * * * *

Industry U Curve – Don't Get Stuck in The Middle!

I have used data from Table 1 below and created two charts to understand how the top publicly listed consumer products companies in India are placed within the consumer products industry.

Table 1:

Company Name	ROCE (EBITDA/ (Networth +Debt))	Net Profit Margin%	Sales (Revenue) in Billions INR 2022-23	PE Ratio
Amrutanjan	16.70%	10.84%	3.86	42.5
Bajaj Consumer	21.20%	13.95%	9.98	17.7
VIP Industries	32.60%	7.26%	20.99	59.4
Gillette India	45.90%	13.69%	24.22	45
Jyothy Laboratories	18.40%	9.64%	24.86	31.8
Emami	23.40%	25.46%	33.43	20.3

P&G Hygiene & Healthcare India	22.60%	14.78%	38.54	79.2
Page Industries	64.30%	13.86%	49.31	69
Colgate Palmolive In	77.90%	20.37%	51.77	41.9
Hatsun Agro	13.70%	2.29%	72.58	118.6
Marico	36.60%	13.33%	97.64	53.8
Dabur	18.40%	14.81%	115.3	53.8
Godrej Consumer	17.40%	12.63%	134.84	60
Tata Consumer	8.20%	8.73%	137.83	60.9
Varun Beverages	32.90%	11.74%	142.39	60.4
Britannia Industries	49.90%	14.24%	163.01	47.9
Nestle India	59.00%	14.34%	176.93	82.9
Patanjali Foods	12.80%	2.83%	303.18	39.3
Asian Paints	31.60%	11.10%	335.26	80.7
Adani Wilmar	14.00%	1.00%	581.85	87.6
HUL	21.30%	16.71%	605.8	60.9
ITC	33.10%	26.00%	698.57	28.7

**Data Source – www.simplywall.st*

EBITDA – Earnings Before Interest, Tax, Depreciation and Amortization

ROCE = Return on Capital Employed

Chart 1: Net Profit% to Sales

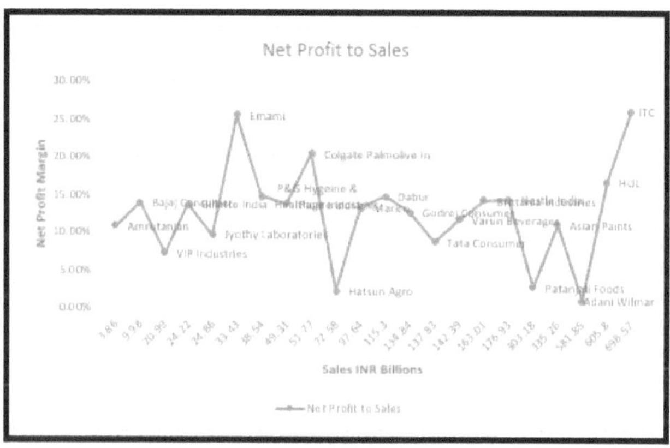

Chart 1 is called an industry U-Curve. Barring a few exceptions, every industry will form a sort of a U-Curve when you plot Sales Value in the X-axis and Net Profit% in the Y-axis. In Chart 1, If you leave out Amrutanjan, VIP Industries and Jyothy Laboratories, you will see a warped U starting from Emami to HUL and ITC. What the U-curve normally says is that the companies that are to the left (The ones with lower sales volume but higher margins) like Emami are the differentiators that have brands that cater to a smaller segment of the market (relatively), but with good net profit margins. The companies to the extreme right are ITC and HUL which are cost leaders (due to economies of scale) that do huge sales volumes and have good profit margins because of the powerful mass market brands. In the middle of the curve companies like Hatsun Agro are neither here nor there, with low profit margins. So as leaders, when we build brands, it is very important to understand which segment of the market we are catering to and build brands accordingly, for maximum emotional leverage and profits. Basically, we should do our best to not get stuck in-between with weak commoditized brands that result in variety seeking consumer behaviour if there is significant difference between brands (i.e. consumers switch brands without much thought) or don't choose the brands at all if there is very little difference between brands and opt for the more visible brands that have better emotional connect and buy them habitually instead of the ones offered by the company stuck in the middle. This brings us to a model called the Henry Assael model below:

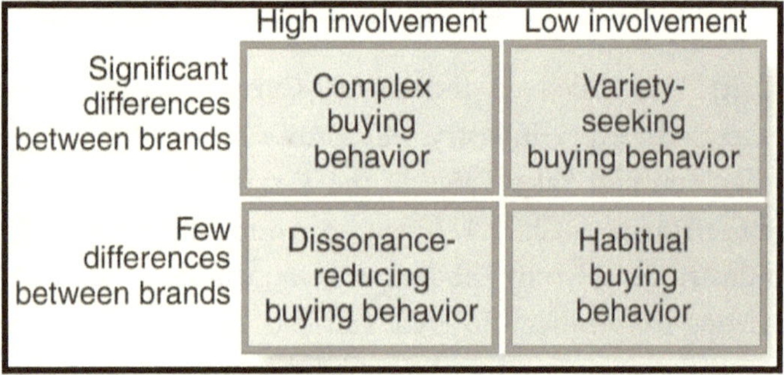

Most Fast-Moving Consumer Goods brands fall in the low-involvement category of consumer behaviour. The challenge for companies is to create strong brands and make consumers buy them habitually, because the FMCG category eventually becomes cluttered with several brands with around 2-3 strong brands. So, the entrepreneur's job is to make the habitual repeat purchase happen whether there are significant differences between the brands or few differences between the brands. The objective is to reduce brand-switching by building MOATS. Powerful brands stand out because they strike a deep emotional chord with their consumers and increase the propensity of the consumer to habitually buy even as the industry offers more and more brands with the same features/benefits. So, we once again note that competing merely on features, benefits or pricing cannot create powerful brands that command a premium over its competitors. An example would be how Marico took on HUL in the hair oil space, when HUL launched NIHAR to compete with Marico's market leader Parachute. In the late 1990s Keki Dadiseth, the then chairman of HUL, seeing the success of Parachute, apparently called Harsh Mariwala (The then Managing Director of Marico) and told him that he would buy Parachute and compensate him with enough to take care of several of his future generations. Harsh Mariwala did the unthinkable and refused to sell Parachute to HUL and doubled down on resources to strengthen the Parachute brand through improved product and packaging quality, increased advertising, and a new tag line 'Shudhtha Ki Shakti'. HUL launched and relaunched Nihar coconut oil several times and finally decided it just couldn't crack the category because of the might of the Parachute brand. It was poetic justice when Marico bought Nihar from HUL for Rs. 220 crores when it put it up for sale in 2005. This made Parachute's market share more than 80% in the perfumed coconut oil category, with improved presence in its weak markets of North and East India!

So, what is Marico's secret formula that keeps the company dominating its categories and building MOATS around its super brands like Parachute and Saffola till date?

As Saurabh Mukherjea writes in his book, Unusual Billionaires since its inception Marico has consistently focussed on the three key factors that helps consumer staples companies build formidable brands and ensure competitive ROCE and growth rates: 1) Maintaining brand leadership, 2) Extending winning brands, 3) Divesting low margin brands. So, in effect Marico has successfully made commodities like coconut oil and edible Safflower oil into super-brands by building an emotional chord with its consumers, making its brands the brands of choice on a habitual basis for its consumers. Another important point to note is Marico's packaging innovation way back in the 80s when coconut oils were sold in Tin cans, they moved to lightweight more attractive plastic bottles. While trade initially had apprehensions, as plastic could be bitten by rats, Marico's innovative circular smooth surface bottles were tested with rats in a cage and demonstrated to trade. This innovative packaging helped Parachute stand out on the shelves and build deep, long-term relationships with trade partners, which became significant assets over the years. The 'Shudta Ki Shakti' tag line stood for purity and trust across geographic markets, whether Parachute coconut oil was used as a cooking oil or hair oil.

Now, let us look at some examples of consumer products that fall in the High Involvement category. Generally, products that are significantly more expensive fall into the High Involvement consumer behaviour category in the Henry

Assael model, because consumers do more research when they have to buy products that are not regular purchases and are significantly more expensive. For example, most high-end flagship mobile phones, have almost similar features. So, if a consumer buys an Apple phone because Apple iPhone has superior design and satisfies the status need for people and has built an emotional chord with the consumer, the consumer will justify in his / her mind of the decision post-purchase, saying Apple products are of superior quality and easier to use. Whether the perceived superior product quality compared to other brands is true or not the consumer justifies the purchase in his mind, and this is called dissonance reducing consumer behaviour. The consumer reassures himself/herself to feel better about spending a premium on the brand of his/her choice. Companies like Apple and Nike have done a brilliant job at building that intimate bond with consumers that consumers don't buy products by comparing features and benefits of their products but buy them because they 'Think Different' or they feel empowered to 'Just Do It'. Such is the power of combining great products with an emotional value-proposition that empowers the consumer to take action.

Now, if we look at buying a car, it would fall into the category of High Involvement with significant differences between brands. In this case the buying behaviour is generally complex because consumers spend a lot of time comparing various brands in their preferred segment. They definitely compare features and benefits but would finally gravitate towards a brand that they have been dreaming of. This purchase decision would involve online research, test drives and discussion with family members about their preferences. For example, Volvo dominates the safety positioning, Mercedes the Luxury Positioning and BMW the freedom, performance, innovation, and luxury positioning. If you watch Volvo ads, most of them would communicate the aspect of Love for family and keeping them safe. Mercedes communicates the luxury and status needs of people while BMW combines the emotion of freedom and exhilaration with luxury. Similarly in the more mass market, Toyota dominates reliability and superior automobiles that move people comfortably. So, again brands that have an emotional association with consumers stand-out as leaders in their segment.

I will leave you with a chart (Chart 2) that maps Return on Capital Employed to Sales for the same top listed fast moving consumer products companies in India, for you to see which ones are utilizing their capital the best:

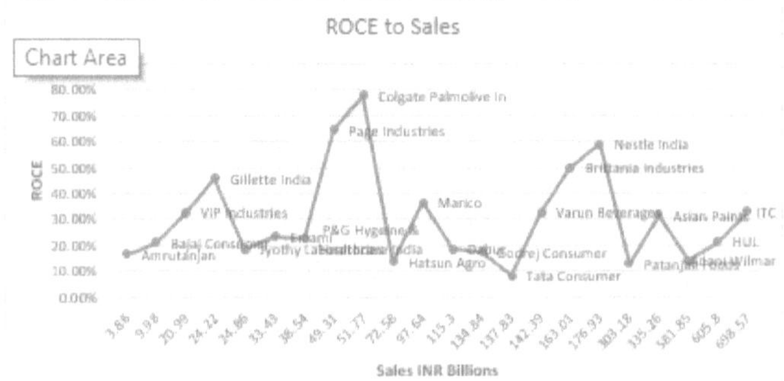

Chart 2

* * * * *

Be Grateful to Those Who Came Before You

When I joined Bril in 2002, I joined as someone who had a lot to learn. I would tell seniors like late Mr. Gopal (My father's right-hand man), Mr. Rao (one of our first salesmen and then inventory manager), late Mr. Chakrapani (Our seniormost Kerala salesman) and late Mr. Ramani (Our Finance head) to teach me all that they knew. I was and am grateful to my grandfather, my father and all the amazing men and women who had kept this brand alive till I was old enough to take charge and manage it. A very important trait for 2nd and 3rd generation entrepreneurs especially, is humility and a deep sense of gratitude for the opportunity that has been handed over to them thanks to the efforts of their family and teams that came before them. Even for leaders joining organizations, acknowledging work done by people who came earlier and building upon that is very important. It's never a good idea to discount the efforts of those who came before you and change things for the sake of change, without realizing the ground realities of the market and why things were happening in a particular way. Having said this, if something is not working, fix and change it for the collective good of the organization and all stakeholders.

While on this topic, I had the opportunity to personally thank and recognize a Karma Yogi of our Organization who was retiring for the second time at the ripe old age of 88, on 1st June 2023 (1st retirement at age 60 was only a formality, as he was immediately back the next day on contract). Mr. Nagarajan has worked with two of our family businesses Bril (Industrial Research Corporation) and Essen and Co since my grandfather's time, growing to become a senior administrative manager. He has had a 63-year stint with our companies! It is people like him who have lived the essence of our value system of Nishkama Karma and have dedicated their professional lives for the organization. I am not saying that people should work in the same organization all their life, but we must recognize those who have done so much even when they could have sought employment elsewhere, probably for a higher pay and perks. The images below are of me and my father, celebrating his last day with my small personal office team in the HO. We shared our celebrations with the entire organization so everyone could wish Mr. Nagaraj well for his retired life.

DIRECTOR

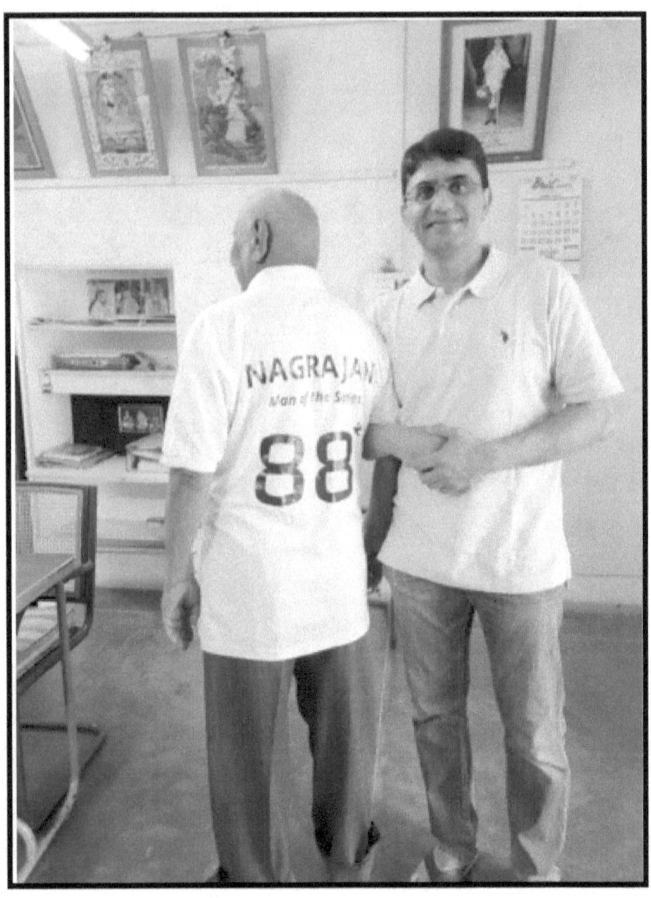
NAGRAJAN
Man of the Series
88*

L-R Back: Padma (Finance Head), Me, Nagendra (My father's and my Executive Assistant), LeelaKumari (Finance), Front L-R: Dr. J.Rajaram (My Father), Mr. Nagaraj (Servant Leader, Karma Yogi)

* * * * *

Managing Change Is Painful

While all this gratitude is very important and sounds rosy, let me tell you that managing change in a heritage organization is no easy task. People may say it is easy to join your own business, you are the boss etc. Let me tell you that nothing works without gaining credibility – even if it is your family business! When I first joined, some of the senior people thought only ink is our product. They would openly tell me that 'non-ink' products are not of interest to them, because they truly believed that only what sells most and what Bril stood for should be sold. There was no thinking about the future or what the market dynamics were, of ball-point pens and gel pens becoming the norm in most states other than Tamil Nadu where Government Schools mandate the use of fountain pens (A good thing for children and the environment). Initially, in my youthful exuberance I would get frustrated and angry and tell my father that this attitude would not help the organization grow – I was a youngster in a hurry. Little did I know that deeply entrenched systems would take time and patience to change. Slowly but surely, I matured, with my father's gentle guidance and unflinching support. This attitude of employees trickled down to trade partners who would merely focus on Inks as that had been their bread and butter for years. I started by meeting employees and explaining to them that Bril is a brand and all products under the umbrella added value to consumers. I told them that it was our duty to look at Bril and its portfolio of consumer products as a whole and communicate the Bril story to trade partners and consumers rather than saying we are just Bril Ink. I showed them my larger vision for Bril and explained to them that their lives would change for the better dramatically if we achieved this vision. While being a one-product company is good, companies like Kodak and NOKIA died from once being dominant only because of denial of a changing market landscape. I brought this to the attention of all employees and trade partners and sensitized them to the fact that we needed their buy-in to take Bril to the next generation of consumers and needed the right attitude to take the product portfolio as a whole to trade and make it reach the end-consumer. This was easier said than done. I recruited managers from FMCG companies instead of those with only stationery experience because those with only stationery experience would continue to sell only Ink and fastest moving products to wholesale. I wanted freshness and a retail focus, and the new managers brought the experience from similar yet different industries like food, confectionery, and other household fmcg products. They were asked to recruit a sales team of 50% stationery and 50% other FMCG experience to bring a balance. All this sounds great on paper, but little did I realize the change management issues I was going to face. The old teams and managers hated the new managers and wouldn't cooperate. The new managers wanted to give credit in the market to boost sales and were at war with the old establishment daily. Both were right and both were wrong, but my life was hell as I had to play the balancing act. This continued till we established norms of never deviating from a 100% advance payment system and making it clear that sales are my number one priority and administration exists to support the sales function. I made it clear that the organization exists because of its customers and the sales we generate by selling to them. Without sales, we could have the best products in the world, but we would die. The painful years saw 3 factory managers quit because they couldn't change their old ways (They were all good people and I still have immense respect for them, and we stay in touch). Any good change in life is painful and once we went through that, we started seeing growth because the team started working with a common objective. It's not that there aren't healthy debates and arguments today, but we have made it clear that there is no room for ego when we fight to solve a problem for the business. Fighting to further the cause of the business and then being friends outside is a very important skill that employees and employers must learn. I use the word fighting for debating, because the debates are loud and passionate, filled with emotion but for the organization's cause. So, in a nutshell, it took a long time for me to be taken seriously, and this happens only when people start seeing results and you walk the talk.

* * * * *

Sales Monitoring and Tech Enablement of Sales

At Bril, we have of late made a major push towards tech enablement of our sales-process and field-force monitoring. While trust plays a crucial role in our organization, we communicate the fact that monitoring is the duty of sales leaders. So, we now have an app designed to help sales reps take orders from retailers and wholesalers and also login their attendance. We can see the position of the salesmen on their routes on Google Maps and track secondary sales being done real time. We can get time spent, product-mix and order-value per outlet to maximize field-force productivity and increase sales per outlet, route, and day. During meetings we discuss product-mix being sold and how to optimize and enhance profitability by selling products with higher gross margins. When we first implemented technology, there was a push-back from the sales team as any change would. The non-performers resisted the change the most, but we communicated the benefits that it would have on individual performance and those that embraced it started selling better and more. This started building confidence in the system amongst sales teams and they started seeing the impact it had on daily performance as daily OKRs and KPIs could be checked real-time. Technology started helping good salesmen do better with the help of data. The issue still on a daily basis is to encourage salesmen to use the data they have on real-time basis to upsell and cross-sell products in every outlet. To also understand which customer buys more of what and how to make him buy SKUs that are more profitable for the organization. I must say that while adoption is good, making people see the value in something that is initially perceived as just a monitoring tool is no easy feat. We as leaders must realize that the people element and culture building is and has to be a daily affair. Day in and day out there will always be people who we have to monitor more, and those who go above and beyond and need zero monitoring. It is our job to identify the self-motivated performers and give them good opportunities to grow faster. This in turn will motivate the slackers to do better. One thing in life is that we can never teach and help those who act like they are asleep. Motivation and the urge to grow professionally and personally must after all come from within and this happens at different stages and under different circumstances for every individual. As a leader we can only create the environment that encourages growth and performance for individual and organizational good.

* * * * *

India's Bootstrapped Poster Children-ZERODHA and ZOHO

While this book is primarily about physical consumer product brands, it will not be complete without a mention of ZOHO and ZERODHA, which are two amazing, bootstrapped software product Unicorns. Sridhar Vembu (ZOHO) and Nithin Kamath and Nikhil Kamath (ZERODHA) have made India proud and shown us what it takes to build, Billion-dollar, profitable businesses with zero external funding and a deep focus on product and user-experience.

Zerodha pioneered the discount broking model in India and is today India's biggest stock broking company. This is no easy achievement. The brand name Zerodha is a combination of Zero and Rodha, which in Sanskrit means barrier. So Zerodha, simply means zero barriers, and its mission is to make trading and investing barrier-free. Nithin Kamath bootstrapped and founded Zerodha in 2010 to overcome the hurdles he faced during his decade long stint as a trader. Nithin started trading with Rs. 8000 at the age of 17. Today, Zerodha has changed the landscape of the Indian broking industry.

Nikhil Kamath, Nithin's brother is an investor and trader and heads financial planning at Zerodha.

Nithin has been trading in the Indian stock market since the age of 17. Nithin attended an engineering college and then went on to become an entrepreneur. During his college years, he spent considerable time trading in the stock market and that forced him to take up a job at a call centre. Hence, he worked at the call centre during the night and saved the daytime for trading. Nithin managed to make decent money but lost it all in the 2001-02 market crash. His experience however landed him his first cheque from a HNI investor who asked him to invest and manage his money. At the same time Nithin got a job with Reliance Money. During his tenure with Reliance, Nithin became one of the best sub-brokers and managed to get reliance some very big clients.

While at Reliance, Nithin felt there was something amiss with respect to customer-experience for traders and investors. Nithin again lost a lot of money during the 2008 financial crash. It was in 2010 that Nithin joined hands with his brother Nikhil to start Zerodha and change the way India trades forever. The beginning however was not easy as Zerodha managed to get only 3000 users in its first year. It was extremely difficult to gain credibility in the market initially as trust is a very important element in the brokerage business, and low-to-no fees got curiosity but little adoption as people perceived something cheap as 'low-quality'. So, to counter this, Nithin and Nikhil did something out-of-the-box and started building a community for traders. Zerodha launched Varsity, a learning module, which has become immensely popular. It also runs Trading Q&A, an active forum were traders and investors, can discuss stock ideas. Then there is 'Z Connect' an interactive blog. Traders started warming up to Zerodha and enjoying the low fees of Rs. 20 per trade irrespective of the trade value as opposed to a percentage charged by other brokers. Investors loved the zero-commission model of Zerodha for equity delivery.

Having built a community, Zerodha invested heavily in technology headed by Kailash Nadh its CTO. The introduction of Kite its mobile app and investing in multiple tech companies, made the user-experience seamless. Nithin and Nikhil have grown from 5 employees in 2010 to 1300 in 2023, 3000 active users to more than 12 million active users in 2023. Zerodha has achieved revenues of Rs. 5500 crores and a PAT of Rs. 2500 crores in FY23, with never spending on any advertising. Nithin, in a podcast stated that Zerodha never recruits from IITs and IIMs: “We've never hired a single person from IIT and IIM till now because we've found it very tough to fit such people within the organisation,” he said during the podcast. He said the graduates from these organizations are “more focused on developing their careers instead of thinking about the growth of the company”. “The thing about IITs and IIMs is that when you're in that kind of environment, you're wired to think about how quickly you can grow in life. This culturally doesn't fit well (at Zerodha) because we can't tell people how quickly they can grow,” Kamath said. He added that for him a candidate's passion matters more than just education. “At least for the core team, the people who do important stuff at Zerodha, we see if they're passionate about the cause. Education doesn't matter,” Kamath noted. What is amazing is that Nithin and Nikhil have managed to retain their core team without even one person leaving, and this in spite of 90% of the team working remotely post the Covid pandemic. This is nothing but intimate leadership on display at the highest level, with unbelievable financial results to back it. So Zerodha never raised any Venture/PE capital, it doesn't spend any money on advertising, stays close to its customers by building a community, has a fantastic product and keeps investing in better technology and takes care of its employees who care about its mission exceedingly well!

Now let us look at ZOHO.

A bootstrapped company founded in Chennai, India and operated today remotely by Founder Sridhar Vembu and engineers scattered across villages in India crossed $1B in revenue in 2022. While Indian IT was focussing on services, Sridhar Vembu and his team were slowly but surely building world-class products for the world from India. This was no easy task as they were taking on giants like Google (Google Workspace) with Zoho Workplace and the likes of Salesforce with ZOHO CRM.

Sridhar is a Princeton graduate and entrepreneur who believed that small & viable businesses can scale & become highly profitable without venture capital funding. Chasing customer satisfaction is more fruitful than chasing investors. Sridhar & ZOHO have achieved this so successfully that it has put India on the IT products map, paving the way for many future entrepreneurs to Build from India, for India and the world.

Sridhar's leadership acumen, nurturing and training grassroots talent and hyper-focus on products that solve customer problems has brought to fruition a simple, yet revolutionary idea that was born in the 1990s, in a small apartment located in the suburbs of Chennai to "Build smart technology to help businesses work better."

It all started back in 1996 when Sridhar's brothers, Kumar Vembu & Shekhar Vembu, along with a Tony Thomas and Sreenivas Kanumuru, created a company called AdventNet, which was a network management company. They built a good technology business but were failing at sales.

In 1996, Tony, Sridhar's senior in college, was working on an SNMP internet protocol software in Silicon Valley and needed somebody to help him sell it to customers. This is when he teamed up with Sridhar. Sridhar joined Zoho–then Advent Network Management–to staff a booth Tony had rented in a trade show, as a salesman.

In 1997, the company made about $350,000 in sales, putting it all back in the R&D unit in Chennai, India. This is when Sridhar and his team were convinced that AdventNet was a "real business". Until then, the founders weren't paying themselves salaries–something Sridhar equated business with. "Customers were actually willing to pay for our product! We found a niche market where customers needed us," Sridhar says.

By 1998, Advent crossed $1 million in sales, and doubled it the next year.

Sridhar realized that the market opportunity was there, and the business was paying employees and was putting food on the table for its promoters. In 1999 Sridhar turned down an offer from a VC firm as it was short-term oriented and required liquidity or an IPO in 8 years. Sridhar was determined to build slow and grow organically without compromising or taking shortcuts to scale.

Unfortunately, in the 2000s business dried up and the telecom market that Advent was serving didn't look like it was going to pick up anytime soon. This was also the time when the dot-com bubble burst and companies were shuttering and going bankrupt left right and centre. In the midst of all the chaos, AdventNet had 3 distinct advantages: 1. Cash in the bank 2. No investors 3. Low operating costs (most of their employees were in India). This was when the company started bringing out products including its cloud division Zoho.com. While the Zoho domain was picked up for USD 5000 from a US-based hospitality startup, it was launched in 2005, Unfortunately this was the same time that there was a difference of opinion between Sridhar and the other cofounders, including his brothers. As a result of the difference in opinion regarding the company strategy, Sridhar's brothers Kumar, & Shekhar, & their friend, Tony left the company. That decision would cost them BILLIONS. Sridhar was the only executive left & said it was the most depressing time of his career. Somehow Sridhar kept the team together and kept building.

Through the years, the company launched several software-as-a-subscription (SaaS) products, for which businesses would pay a certain fee for a year. It launched one of its most popular products, a customer relationship management (CRM) software—Zoho CRM—in November 2005. This was followed by several other products such as Mail, Writer, Sheet, Show, Creator, Docs, and Meeting—which put it in competition with some of the leading software giants across the world. Having built a lot more products, entered bigger markets, and found a lot more customers in successive years, Advent was rebranded as Zoho Corporation in 2009. The biggest hit came with their SaaS Project Management tool. After that there was no looking back for Sridhar and Zoho.

Now comes the coolest part. As they scaled, there was a lack of quality talent to build products in India. ZOHO didn't want to increase costs by recruiting talent from abroad. Instead, Sridhar dug deep and decided to recruit from tier 2 cities, towns and even villages of India. Now recruiting would be the easy part, but Sridhar had to train these people to deliver top-notch software products that compete with the best in the world. So, ZOHO University was born and started offering FREE engineering education to hungry youngsters from rural India. There are many stories of security guards and daily wage earners going from barely surviving to software engineers thanks to ZOHO University!

During the course of this program, the students are not charged anything but instead, they are given a basic stipend per month. Once they complete the program, they are hired by Zoho. Today, Zoho has 10,000+ employees & the majority of them come from this program. If this is not intimate leadership, what is?

Zoho has gone on to launch 35+ business apps like Zoho Mail, Zoho CRM, and Zoho WorkDrive. Despite the current economy, they recently crossed a BIG milestone. $1B in revenue. A 77% increase in annual revenue from 2020.

Just before the pandemic lockdown, Sridhar made his workforce 100% remote and went back to his village in

Tenkasi, himself. So, ZOHO now recruits hungry talent from remote villages and upskills them. This is a win-win model as rural-folk now get unimaginable software-engineering jobs and financial security without having to migrate to big cities. The business operates at significantly lower costs when compared to competition in bigger cities in India and more so than those in Silicon Valley! This cost advantage is passed on to customers who lap up Zoho products. As I type this, Google Workspace has increased their price, and I am considering shifting to ZOHO Workplace for my organization because it is almost 1/10th the cost! That's a huge saving month on month for any company!

Sridhar shows us that you don't need to be in Silicon Valley or raise BILLIONS of dollars of VC/PE funding to create a successful technology products business.

ZOHO and Sridhar like Zerodha are an inspiration to millions of entrepreneurs like us, because India needs more real, profitable businesses like this to catapult it into the big league globally. We should stop celebrating fundraising at obscene valuations and start rooting for the entrepreneurs who risk it all and build truly enduring world-class businesses that add value to India and all stakeholders.

* * * * *

What I Think About Valuations and a Quick Lesson for New Founders

Over the years I have tried to study and understand how companies are valued. Valuation till around 30 years ago used to be a largely quantitative exercise with some assumptions of growth rates, assumption of a company being a going concern forever etc, along with some subjective goodwill for intangible assets like brand equity and trade relationships. So it was primarily a combination analysis of the balance sheet: The Assets and Liabilities of a company to calculate its net worth (Owner's Equity (Net worth)= Assets-Liabilities) and discounting future free-cash-flows to the present value using a reasonable discount rate (Company's cost of equity capital) that a person investing would desire plus the terminal value (Which is calculated using the last value of Free Cash Flow, a growth rate to perpetuity and the discount). If debt and equity are used for funding the discount rate would be the weighted average cost of capital. Equity investors have to get a risk premium over and above the risk-free rate of bonds/FDs if they have to consider investing in the company. For the company, this discount rate is its equity cost of capital or cost of capital if there is no debt involved. This cost of capital or the investor's required rate of return should be less than the return the company can generate with the capital raised. So, if the discount rate is 15% (7% more than the risk-free bond/FD rate of 8%), then the company should generate returns higher than this discount rate (cost of capital) to add value. So, the IRR or Internal Rate of Return of a company is the discount rate at which the sum of all future cashflows of a project is equal to the initial investment in the project (In other words the NPV or Net Present Value = Sum of FCFs discounted by IRR minus Original Cash Outflow or Investment = 0). **This IRR should be greater than 15%, if that (15%) was used as the discount rate to calculate the company's post-money valuation.** So, in other words, the Net Present Value of any project undertaken by the company should be positive if the sum of all future Free Cash Flows from the project are discounted by the cost of capital which is 15% in this case and subtracted from the original investment or cash outflow.

So, Company Valuation = FCF Year 1/ (1+R) + FCF Year 2/ (1+R)^2 ......FCF Year n /(1+r)^n + Terminal Value (Terminal Value is computed as [FCFn x (1 + g)] / (R – g))

- FCFn = free cash flow for the last forecast period
- g = terminal growth rate
- R= Discount rate (which is the return the equity investors required if there is no debt, or Weighted Average Cost of Capital if there is debt and equity capital in a company). In our example R = 15% or 0.15

Now assuming this company has only equity capital and its cost of capital is 15%, it has to generate returns of more than 15% to create value. Hence the Internal rate of return must be greater than 15%

So, when we calculate IRR using excel or the trial-and-error method manually we will notice that NPV or net present value should be zero only when IRR is > 15%. If less, then the company is eroding value.

NPV = – Original Investment + FCF Year 1/ (1+IRR) + FCF Year 2/ (1+IRR)^2 ……FCF Year n /(1+IRR)^n = 0

Now, if we discount future cashflows of a project by the cost of capital (R) which is 15%, the Net Present Value (NPV) should be positive in order to show that the project is generating more money than the cost of capital of 15%

NPV = – Original Investment + FCF Year 1/ (1+R) + FCF Year 2/ (1+R)^2 ……FCF Year n /(1+R)^n

The above NPV should be positive.

I will give you a very simplified purely theoretical Rs. 100 example to make you understand the logic behind DCF Valuation, without any terminal value (i.e., we will assume the company is run only for one year and then closed).

Let us say a company has Rs. 80 in cash and Owner's equity and 8 shares outstanding (I.e., Rs. 10 per share X 8 shares). Now the company is in a business that can make 30% returns. So Rs. 80 will become Rs. 80X1.3 = Rs. 104 FCF after 1 year. Now, let us say the company needs Rs. 100 for a project and an investor wants to invest Rs. 20 into this business for a 20% return.

The company will now have Rs. 100 cash and the Free Cash Flows in Year One at 30% IRR will be Rs. 130

Now at what valuation does the investor enter since the return of 20% he wants will be the discount rate R?

Rs. 130/(1+R) = Rs. 130/1.2 = Rs. 108.333333 (Post Money Valuation)

The investor gets Rs. 20/108.333333 = 18.4615%

While he invests 20% of the Rs. 100 capital he gets only 18.4615% because he wants only 20% return while the company makes 30% return on invested capital.

Now how are the new shares allotted to the investor?

8 shares / ((100-18.4615)/100) ➔ 8 /0.815385 * 0.184615 = 1.81132 shares for Rs. 20 invested.

Rs. 20/1.81132 shares = Rs. 11.0417 per share. You know that 1.81132 shares is purely for theoretical purposes, right? 😉

Total shares outstanding post investment = 8 + 1.81132 = Rs. 9.81132

Rs. 11.0417 per share X (8+1.81132) shares after investment = Rs. 11.0417 X 9.81132 = Rs. 108.333 which is the post-money valuation (Same as what we got using the DCF method above). The notional pre-money valuation would now be Rs. 11.0417/share X 8 shares pre money = Rs. 88.3336, though the actual equity capital before the fund raise was only Rs 80 (8 shares X Rs. 10). Don't worry too much about this notional pre-money valuation.

Now how do you explain the fact that the investor gets only 20% return while the company makes 30% using the total invested capital of Rs. 100 post-money raise?

First let us look at the percentage of the Free Cash Flow that the investor gets by virtue of owning 18.4615% after year 1. He gets 18.4615% X Rs. 130 = Rs. 24. How much did he invest? Rs. 20, how much does he get after year one? Rs. 24. That is 20% return, which he wanted!

Another way to look at it is that the investor invests 20% of the Rs. 100 equity capital but gets only 18.4615% . This means he gets 20%-18.4615% = 1.5385% less

1.5385% of 100% = x% of 20% ?

X= 1.5385/20X100 = 7.6925%

So, he loses 7.6925% of his investment the minute he invests and also forgoes the 30% return that the 7.6925% gets for the company. 30% of 7.6925% = 2.28885%. So, he loses 7.6925+2.28885% or 7.695%X1.3 = 10%. So, of the 30% the company makes, he forgoes 10% return and retains 20%. The promoter on the other hand invests Rs. 80 or 80% of the capital and gets 81.5385%. 81.5385% of Rs. 130 cashflow is Rs. 106. So Rs. 80 becomes Rs. 106 which is a 32.5% return by virtue of what the investor foregoes.

Now no matter what the company does, the company should aim to get returns more than its 20% cost of capital. This is a super-simplistic way of looking at it, but as a non-finance guy, when I first started off studying valuations, this is how I wrapped my head around DCF, pre and post-money valuations. Hope I didn't confuse you too much 😊

I have broadly explained the above for the benefit non-finance founders, but the above quantitative methods along-with subjective/qualitative elements like assumed growth rates and goodwill for brand equity, distribution depth/relationships were used to value companies till around 30 years ago. This valuation method still works well for mature companies with predictable Free Cash Flows, tangible assets and liabilities and some goodwill or standing in the market. Now this worked well till the tech companies and new-age startups came into vogue in Silicon Valley USA, where founders had phenomenal ideas that would go on to change the world, but no real numbers. Now, there was a dilemma among traditional valuers because they did not understand this game. So, in came the angel investors and venture capitalists, who invested based on their gut about the market potential of the story and idea being communicated and the credibility/skillset of the founding team. This was a truly heady period because no bank would give debt to these startups without collaterals, and they needed real-life angels to change the world! So, this started a trend of HNIs (High Net worth Individuals) and funds with HNIs as their investors funding zero revenue ideas at valuations their risk-appetite permitted them to, based on the founding team's conviction of giving them huge returns and the thrill of finding the next world-changing idea. The investors would take huge risks on their disposable capital in the hope of a huge return on their investment in the mid to long term. Without this VC ecosystem, we would never have the current generation's super-companies FANMAG (Facebook, Amazon, Netflix, Microsoft, Apple, and Google). Now add Tesla, Uber, Nykaa, Paytm, Zomato etc to the mix of listed Venture-Funded companies in the US and India. So, as Dr. Ashwath Damodaran, valuation guru so beautifully says, for a new company and a high-growth early-stage startup, the story is more important than the numbers, provided the organization has the business model and unit economics to subsequently make money (This is crucial). For mature-growth companies the valuation slowly moves more to the numbers than the story as the market finds it hard to value nimbleness of a company to keep coming up with earth shattering innovations. Now for example, who would have known that Microsoft would lead the AI revolution with its $10 Billion bet and partnership with OpenAI? So, the market invariably reacts and factors these things into the valuation once there is excitement about a future game-changing technology play by an established company.

Finally, there are companies that are on the decline, as Ashwath Damodaran says in a talk, which are better off returning money to shareholders through dividends and share buy-backs, because the capital can no longer be used well by these companies. These companies that are on decline should generally be valued purely based on their balance sheet as their future business is uncertain. While I believe consumer-products companies that achieve a reasonable scale and brand-love have long lifecycles of 50-100+ years and can still be relevant if managed well (and with lots of luck), most tech companies have 7–10-year lifecycles in today's ever-changing world. So, the company-lifecycle itself is shrinking as Ashwath Damodaran rightly says.

Having said all this, I am neither for or against companies raising huge capital based on great stories, but what the market is telling us clearly today is that the stories are becoming just that – stories. We should never go back to the days of the dotcom bust and economic carnage in 2001 when companies were valued based on eyeballs. It's no longer eyeballs, but human greed seems to find new metrics to cover up the naked Emperor. This is where the VC and startup ecosystem start losing credibility, because many of the startups raising money at obscene valuations today are just not earth-shattering businesses that they claim to be. What's worse is that these companies don't seem to have any clue about how they are going to become profitable and the huge valuations during multiple rounds of fund-raise, make the company so bloated that when a loss-making company goes in for an IPO, the poor retail investor sits on the biggest losses. This is where I draw the line and ask entrepreneurs to focus on building an enduring, profitable, cash flowing business (that of course may have a lifecycle and maybe eventually sold or die in its natural course). Raise the money if you wish to, but don't raise money at valuations that will come back to bite you when business doesn't come in as per your excel sheet projections. Trust me, it's not GMV that is important – it is your real revenues, cash flows and profits (or definitive path/plan to profits) that count. If VCs are not investing because your valuation is low and the idea doesn't address a big enough market according to them, look elsewhere for your money. Be very clear to tell investors that you wish to think about being profitable from day 1, even if it means you will not necessarily make those profits in the first few years. So, as we all understand, valuation is an art more than a science, but it shouldn't become a passing the parcel game, as it has these days.

* * * * *

Mind Your Quadrant

Shade Zahrai a leading motivational speaker and leadership coach explains effective leadership by putting people in a humanness-matrix. I rephrase that as Intimate leadership as this is exactly what I speak about as intimate leadership. I will give you my take on the matrix below as it simplifies where leaders should aspire to be.

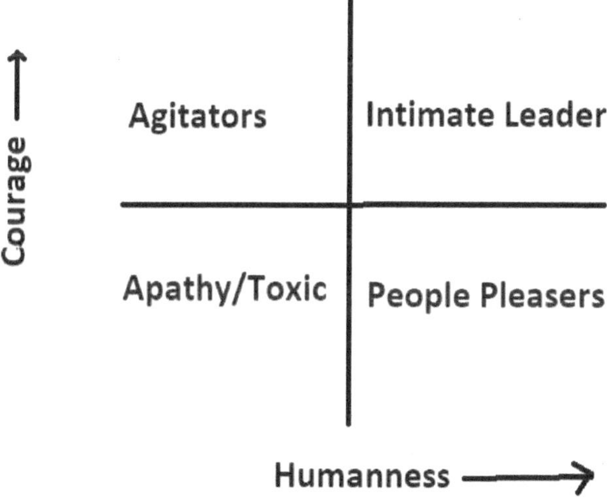

Very simply put, people who are high on courage and low on humanness, tend to reprimand and agitate people without understanding how it affects them. They tend to reprimand publicly and rag to show their power over people. They tend to be full of themselves and have very little emotional quotient. Such people may produce results but find it hard to keep the team motivated and backing them.

People who are low on Courage and Low on Humanness tend to be toxic and are normally the ones who spread office gossip and politicize things to gain importance. Their lack of courage and humanness makes them unfit for a leadership role as they are negative and pull people down.

Those who are high on Humanness but low on Courage, have the tendency to want to be liked by everyone. They are people pleasers and are seldom able to take tough decisions that are right for the team and organization. These people try to be 'fair' to everyone and end up losing the good performers as they start feeling short-changed. Leadership is not a popularity contest. Leaders exist to help teams and organizations achieve common objectives and must be courageous enough to recognize and incentivise those who do well more than those who are average. Leaders should have the courage to let go of people who are unethical or spoiling the sacrosanct organizational culture. Leadership is tough and good leaders are seldom concerned about being liked by everyone.

Now, Intimate leaders are those who are high on Courage and high on Humanness. These people have the courage to take tough decisions but do so with utmost empathy. These people are able to perform in an egoless manner most of the time and are first to say sorry if they make a mistake. Intimate leaders put people (whether coworkers, shareholders, or customers) at the centre of everything they do. They are ready to take feedback and change their decisions if someone else has a better approach or idea. They are firm and decisive, yet flexible. They understand that an organization and brand is after all the effect of people serving people, and that without motivated employees, achieving satisfied customers is impossible. So, this is the quadrant that we must all try to align to on a daily basis. It is not a cakewalk, but we must be aware of our transgressions and try to keep moving back to this quadrant even if we slip into any of the other quadrants momentarily.

* * * * *

Do Not Be in a Hurry – Patience and Focus Compounds Like Crazy!

On June 13th, 2023, shares of MRF (Madras Rubber Factory – MRF Ltd.) touched Rs. 1,00,000 (Rupees 1 Lakh) and made history of becoming India's first company to have a six-figure share price. In April 1993, the share price was Rs. 11. The company never split its shares and issued bonus shares only twice, so in effect Rs. 11 has become Rs. 1 lakh in 30 years. This is a whopping 908991% absolute returns to patient shareholders. This is 35.5% CAGR (Compound Annual Growth Rate) over 30 years. The Sensex in the same period has given approximately 18% CAGR, an FD gives around 8%! MRF has given a compounding rate of almost double of the entire Sensex Index in the 30-year period! So, if a person had invested Rs. 1,10,000 in MRF Shares in 1993 and held on to them, it would have become Rs. 100 Crores in June 2023!

While we are not talking about investing, in this book, we are talking about leadership and how to build world-class, profitable, cash flowing and enduring consumer product brands that also reflect in a company's share price, if publicly listed. MRF is a world-class tyre brand, and it wasn't built in a day! Too many founders these days are in a hurry to scale at any cost and exit. While I pass no judgement on that approach, my personal preference is businesses that endure and add value for several decades or even centuries. MRF was started by K. M. Mammen Mappillai laying its foundation in 1946 as a modest toy balloon manufacturing unit in Tiruvottiyur, Chennai (then Madras). However, it was not long before MRF set its sights on greater horizons, venturing into the production of tread rubber a mere six years later. Since then, MRF has been almost 100% focused on making world-class tyres for two-wheelers and four wheelers. By 1956 MRF had garnered 50% market share in the category as stated in its website. MRF as a brand and its strongman carrying the tyre logo (Depicting the tag line 'Tyres with Muscle') have been etched in our minds and collective consciousness depicting strength, durability, and superior quality. MRF innovated and kept up with innovations like radial tyres, tubeless tyres etc. The company ranked 13th in the world in the world's best tyre brands list*.

MRF today clocks Rs. 230 billion (Rs. 23000 crores) and PAT of Rs. 7.7 billion (Rs. 770 Crores), coming in just behind Apollo tyres which recently overtook MRF as the number one tyre company in terms of revenues. Apollo does Rs. 245 billion (Rs. 24500 Crores) in revenues and Rs. 11 billion (Rs. 1100 crores) in profit after tax. These are figures for the financial year-ended March 31st, 2023. Now, despite not being the biggest tyre company in India, ask anyone which is the best tyre company in India and pat comes the answer – MRF! This goes to show the power of focus, innovation and getting intimate with consumers through sponsorship of cricket bats of legends like Sachin Tendulkar and now Virat Kohli. Back in 2001 MRF signed a historic Rs. 100 crores deal to make Sachin their brand ambassador. The subtle connection between the quality and strength of these great players' bats and the players' reliability to depict the reliability and strength of MRF tyres is marketing genius. Even before this, in 1988, MRF setup MRF Pace Foundation with Dennis Lillee to nurture pace bowlers from India and abroad. It also went on to bring the 6th World Boxing championship to Mumbai further etching its 'Tyres With Muscle' brand positioning. In 1989, MRF enhanced customer-intimacy by becoming the first tyre company to launch a wheel-care complex called MRF Tyredrome in Chennai. While MRF did lose focus slightly by partnering with Hasbro to launch Funskool toys in India, it has managed to keep the business separate and not get diverted from its core tyre business.

The message from the MRF story for founders and entrepreneurs like us, is that being in a hurry and chasing the next best thing seldom builds powerful brands. While we live in a world of instant gratification and everyday there is news of startup-founders burning through cash, there is never any shortcut to sustained success in business. Brand building is a marathon, a real game of focus, persistence, and perseverance.

* * * * *

Just Do It – Take That Risk Your Gut Says Will Be a Gamechanger

I am a total and complete India-lover and would never dream of being or working in any other country other than this great country. However, if there was one time I would have loved to work in the US for a few years, it would have been the heady 1980s when consumer brands like NIKE were being built. Sadly, I was too young in the 80s, to do so. I sort of lived the emotion while watching the movie AIR on Amazon Prime, about the historic signing of Michael Jordan and the creation of the emotion and phenomenon that is Air Jordan. While success has many fathers, failure is an orphan, so I will go by what the movie depicts as what really happened, because everyone wants credit for the Jordan deal now.

On a regular evening in 1984 Sonny Vaccaro, the sports marketing executive of the basketball division is watching replays of basketball games on television using recorded VCR Tapes. His mind is anxious because NIKE's budget for basketball is small because so far NIKE has made its name only for running shoes. Sonny and his team have no idea how to split the small budget of USD 250,000 per year among three players. While they had been betting small on different players, nothing so far had yielded any results. This evening, suddenly a three-pointer by an NBA rookie caught Vaccaro's eye. He replays the shot several times, his gut telling him that something about this 21-year-old kid is special. The next day he goes to Phil Knight the founder and CEO of Nike and tells him that he wants a higher budget. Phil says a straight out no and says there is no way he can convince the board to increase the budget for a non-priority (at that time) division like basketball. After the meeting Sonny calls David Falk, Michael Jordan's agent and tells him he wants Jordan. Falk laughs and mocks him saying Jordan doesn't like NIKE and he would most likely go with Converse or Adidas. He also indicated that nothing short of USD 250000 would work.

The next day, Vaccaro tells Rob Strasser, Phil's right-hand marketing executive that he wants to bet the entire annual basketball marketing budget of USD 250,000 on Jordan instead of three average players. Rob Strasser thinks he is crazy and says Phil will never agree. He also tells him that his and the team's jobs could be on the line if the deal failed. Vaccaro still gives it a shot with Phil and tells him something very important. He tells Phil that he (Phil) didn't build NIKE by being safe. He goes on to say that NIKE does almost USD 1 Billion dollars in revenues because of the risks Phil and his team took. Phil says Vaccaro is crazy and disses him. Sonny doesn't take no for an answer and drives straight to Michael Jordan's house and somehow gets Deloris Jordan to listen to him. He tells her that Converse and Adidas will not do justice to Michael and that he would be just another player for them. He goes on to say that Michael is special, and NIKE understands that. An emotional pitch that makes Deloris take note.

Falk can't believe Vaccaro bypassed him and met Jordan's mother directly. He says there is no way NIKE would get the deal because Jordan doesn't fancy NIKE shoes, which were perceived as running shoes back then. Phil hears about Vacarro's meeting with Deloris and relents saying they would bet the entire basketball budget on Jordan. After meeting Adidas and Converse, Deloris, Jordan's mother realizes that what Vacarro said that they would say was indeed true. Adidas had a leadership issue because Adolf (Adi) Dassler had passed away and the board was pulling in different directions without one leader who could bring the team together. Converse had greats like Magic Johnson and Michael Jordan would just be one more in the list as Vacarro had told Deloris. After the meetings, Deloris confirms their meeting with NIKE. Over the weekend Vacarro gets Peter Moore the designer and creative director of NIKE to design a shoe specifically for Jordan. Peter Moore understands this better than anyone and says, "we need a shoe that is designed for one man but speaks to a mass audience by designing the most beautiful shoe known to mankind." Vaccaro wants a red shoe but NBA's rule states that at least 51% of the shoe should be white. When Peter tells him this rule, Rob Strasser (NIKE's Marketing Executive) who is also in the meeting, says why not have more red, lots of red and that NIKE will pay the fines. He goes onto say that the fines by NBA can be made into a commercial that says NBA fines Michael Jordan for being too colourful! This is marketing genius at its best! Make an emotional aspirational connection with future young basketball players by signing on an up-and-coming superstar NBA player who they believe is going to break all records, make a special shoe for him that stands out and make noise about the fines NBA slaps on him to make more people buy the shoes to feel like they are Jordan! Jordan, this shoe, and NIKE were going to create history, and it's almost as though the core team handling this knew something big is about to happen. Such is the power of the human gut and emotions! No data, AI or research in the world can match this rawness in predicting the future of magic that was going to unfold because of this deal.

The Jordan's arrive on Monday and the team pitches. While the video is playing, Sonny asks them to turn it off and speaks directly to Jordan and his mom. He makes an emotional speech about how Jordan will be built up and put on a pedestal as he was going to be a star and a true American story. Vaccaro tells him that he will be built up and will have to live up to it day in and day out. He goes on to say that when he goes up, he will get pulled right down, get hurt, humiliated, and beaten like it always happens to celebrities and great athletes. He goes on to say that what will define Jordan is what makes him rebuild and get up again after he is brought to the ground and attacked. The classic line of the emotional pitch is that **'A Shoe is Just a Shoe until somebody steps into it. Then it has meaning'**. He goes on to says that the rest of us just want a chance to touch that greatness – we need you to get into those shoes, not so you have meaning in your life but so we have meaning in ours. A raw, emotional, and truthful pitch! They hand over the deal papers to the family and the Jordan's leave.

Days pass and Howard Tucker another NIKE executive who was a part of the deal calls Sonny to tell him that ADIDAS had matched the offer, and that Michael Jordan would most likely accept the offer. However, after a few minutes the phone rings and Jordan's mother comes on the line. She tells Sonny that Michael would accept the deal but on one condition, that NIKE pays Michael Jordan a percentage of the revenue of every Air Jordan shoe sold anywhere in the world for life! Sonny says that the industry doesn't work like that and people like us don't get to make the rules. Deloris's master negotiation skills and absolute belief in her son make her say that he is going to be the all-time greatest player in NBA ever and that he needs to get compensated for the meaning he brings to the NIKE brand. She says he has to live up to the aspirations of millions of young children who would buy that shoe to become like Jordan. Vaccaro says people like us, like Jordan, we work for a living and don't get to own anything, and we must take the best we can get. Deloris doesn't relent and the call ends. When Vaccaro tells Phil, to his disbelief Phil says let's do it, 'cos NIKE wasn't built playing safe!'

I have written the real story of this epic deal as also shown in the movie AIR because, Air Jordan till date represents USD 4 Billion in revenue for NIKE. Michael Jordan went onto become the Greatest of All Time Basketball player and the first athlete to breach USD 1 Billion Dollars in Net worth, primarily due to his mother's phenomenal deal she struck for him with Nike. Jordan is said to make USD 400 Million in passive income from the revenue share with NIKE. Michael Jordan is unequivocal that his coach George Ravelling was one of the main reasons he agreed to sign with NIKE. Peter Moore replaced the NIKE logo with the Jordan flying silhouette to create another masterpiece logo.

The message to all of us is that entrepreneurship is majorly about gut instinct. While we can run also ran businesses, it is our gut that propels us to great decisions. We must learn not to silence that inner voice that tells us it is going to work. At the same time if our gut says no but data says otherwise, we really need to think it through, because in my opinion the human brain and gut instinct (if we are sensitive to it) is far superior to any data. Great businesses aren't bult by managers who merely manage, but those who defy all odds and take that big swing.

* * * * *

Frugality Should Be in Your Organization's DNA

When I think frugality, I immediately think of my father. For 40 long years, my father would travel every two weeks for 2-3 days to our Chennai factory. He would only travel by the night mail both ways and book an upper berth in the second-class compartment. It is not that he couldn't afford to fly or take the day train. He just liked doing this and was very comfortable. He made no bones about it and never felt he was doing anything great, but I grew up seeing him. It is another thing that I tried to do what he did and ended up groggy the whole day next day. So, over a period of time, I realized I wasn't cut out for the night mail and shifted to taking the Shatabdi or flying. The best part was that my father did not expect me to do what he did, but today I know the value of frugality for a company. I hire managers who are frugal and that trickles down to the entire organization. None of my employees have airs about being managers or have any entitlement issues. They are all equally comfortable taking trains, buses, or flights (in the rare occasions when necessary) to visit markets. While founders and leaders need not be frugal to the extent of facing hardships, I am shocked to see the new trend of investor-money paying for founders' fancy cars, homes, and lifestyle when the company hasn't made a single dollar in profits. The sheer carelessness while dealing with other people's money is seen in today's startup world where VCs raise someone else's money, invest it without proper due diligence in a multitude of companies like they are gambling and the founders spend the raised money like there is no tomorrow, to raise more money! Where is value being created when people are selling a product that costs Rs. 100 at Rs. 101 by spending Rs. 300 to achieve that sale? I sometimes wonder whether I have become old school and whether I have forgotten what it is to build a business. I am sure anyone trying to build a bootstrapped, economically viable business will have these doubts because all the media attention goes to the newest paper Unicorn in town. Many of the 'angel investors' on popular TV programs are people who have never achieved profitability in their own companies but have made a fortune by paying themselves more than market salaries from investor money! Please trust me, with the kind of scams that are tumbling out of the funded-startup closet, it is clear that entrepreneurship can never be a get-rich-quick scheme. It is a grueling, frustrating, yet highly rewarding long-term game.

* * * * *

Why did We Launch Home Care Products? Were We Losing Focus?

Many people believe that we should have stuck to stationery and not entered the highly cluttered Home Care FMCG category. Sometimes life throws you curve balls, and you must do something for your company to survive. While I always imagined Bril to be a complete household consumer products brand and company, little did I realize that a move into the Home Care category would become one of survival for the business.

When Covid struck in 2020, schools were closed for 2 years, and the non-essential FMCG stationery business was hit by almost 70%. Mind you, that was our core business contributing to 90% of our revenues. Being a well-established 56-year-old brand then, we did the unthinkable job, with God's grace, of not laying off a single employee and paying full salaries for 2 years despite having negligible business. It was in these dire times that I had my thinking cap on and also customers, employees and trade came forward to suggest Bril launch some products in the essential Home or Personal care space to stay afloat and also help trade partners stay in business. This is when we zeroed in on the Home Care Health and Hygiene category to be able to keep our sales teams engaged and productive bringing in some revenues at least. Obviously to get trials and build on existing consumer trust, we decided to use our highly recognizable brand Bril which had tremendous brand equity amongst millions of consumers in practically every household in Southern India (and off late in many households pan India through our online business). With our distribution strength Bril has even been able to open up new channels in stationery shops during the lockdowns and helped small businesses do some business during critical times. Some such shops continue to sell Bril's Home Care products. We appealed to consumers and our social media followers to help us stay in business by supporting our Home Care range which too was 100% Made in India and Made for India. Slowly but surely, this category started picking up and gave at least an additional boost to the morale of the team during the very difficult two years during Covid. While almost every industry other than medical suffered during covid, we were in one of the worst affected industries that was down in the dumps for 2 whole years till school reopened. So, was the entry into the Home Care category planned and strategic? The answer is an absolute NO. Would we like to build on the opportunity that came our way due to our core business being hit so badly? The answer is a resounding YES! Business and life are so unpredictable, and Covid showed us that it is imperative for us to have a well-diversified portfolio that goes into the same households, through the same channels. While this was a brand extension, I look at it as a consumer products line extension for us. So, what about lack of FOCUS? Our focus is and will always be consumer products. I am 100% convinced that as long as we don't diversify to unrelated categories and can leverage the strength of our brand (either as is or as prefix / suffix) and distribution channels, we are focussed. As an organization, we mustn't spread resources too thin, but must also be sufficiently diversified to avoid the downside of being so focussed in one category that we can go out of business due to disruption or force majeure events like a pandemic. Having said all this, finally it boils down to God's grace and luck. Like we have no clue when we will die, we have no idea what the lifetime of a business is. We can only do our best and leave the rest to the Almighty.

* * * * *

Where's the Real Bharath, and How to Serve It?

The new buzzword in the startup world today is TAM or Total Addressable Market or Total Available Market. Every entrepreneur starts with 1.4 billion people in mind and makes projections of revenues based on these numbers. But wait, does your product really address this entire market? Forget the other buzzwords SAM (Serviceable Addressable Market or your target audience) and SOM (Serviceable Obtainable Market or the percentage of SAM your offerings can realistically achieve). First and foremost, I would like to tell you that if you wish to look at TAM as 1.4 billion people you should have a product that really adds value to the entire country. Do you have products at Rs. 5 and Rs. 10? Will you really be able to match the price-performance envelope that is needed to capture the rural market? CavinKare did this with sachets way back in 1983, but now we are no longer in 1983, and the clutter is insane. Do you have any innovation that can cater to rural India? Can you really take on the giants like HUL, P&G, Marico, Emami, Dabur etc? If your answer to these questions is no, then your TAM is wrong. Most funded startups are bleeding and founder-led unethical behaviour, like cooked books, inflated and falsified revenues etc is a result of Venture Capitalists seeking obscene growth based on a wrong Total Available Market. The whole thing is flawed, and both the VCs and founders are to be blamed for this kind of mess.

Now coming back to addressing Bharath. How can you do it? Enter with a mindset to serve the poorest consumer, the upwardly mobile aspiring consumer, and the most affluent consumer. When you do this, you come directly in competition with the giants with super brands. But the only way out is to think hard and deep about unsolved problems and service / products that the biggies have not addressed yet. A brand is finally in the minds of the consumer and every consumer builds your brand for you based on his/her perception of your brand, based on usage of the product and service offered. So, the key element is to see what product you wish to sell and study if that product is needed by every person in the country (I mean that is the real Bharath you are after right?). Once that is established, you will need to see if you can sell a version or SKU of that product at Rs. 1, Rs.2, Rs. 5, Rs. 10, Rs. 20 and Rs. 25! These numbers are golden numbers for mass-appeal consumer brands. Why do you think HUL and P&G also have Rs. 10 detergent powder sachets? Why do the top FMCG companies have Rs. 1 / Rs. 3 shampoo sachets (Look up Clinic Shampoo Sachets)? Why does ParleG, India's highest selling biscuits have a Rs. 5 SKU with 4 biscuits and a pack that has 1 KG of biscuits at Rs. 1398? That's the only way to address Bharath as a whole and be insanely successful while doing it! Why do we at Bril have Rs. 5 Ball Point Pens, Rs. 20/25 Fountain Pens, Re. 1 erasers, Rs. 10 Detergent Powder and Liquid Detergent and fountain pens that are Rs. 999 and 1 litre fmcg bottles that are priced above Rs. 100 and even Rs. 299? But can we serve the entire Bharath with a Rs. 7990 Brilrider AF or a

Rs. 9990 Brilrider Flight AF? No, right? The Brilrider's TAM is limited to the upper-middle-class, upwardly mobile and affluent demographic. Now this is the mistake most VC funded entrepreneurs are making and sadly failing. Please understand that if a person is earning Rs. 25000 per month they belong to the top 10% wage earners in India? If a person has a net worth of Rs. 1.45 crores they belong to the top 1% wealthiest people in the country! So, most D2C startups are literally not even addressing the 31% middle class population of India. Shocking right? As shocking as it may be, this is the harsh truth of why most startups fail to scale and even if they do, they will probably never be profitable, because they never factored in the consumer in real Bharath, but projected revenues with them in mind. They merely use them as a statistic to raise funds.

On the other hand, just recently Isha Ambani who heads Reliance Retail launched Tira a beauty products brand. Isha Ambani, Executive Director, Reliance Retail Ventures Limited, said in her interview with Economic Times, "We are excited to bring the Tira experience to our Indian customers. With Tira, we aim to break down barriers in the beauty space and democratize beauty for consumers across segments. Our vision for Tira is to be the leading beauty destination for accessible yet aspirational beauty, one that is inclusive and one that harbours the mission of becoming the most loved beauty retailer in India." If you notice, Reliance understands real Bharath better than anyone else. She uses the words 'accessible, yet aspirational' and 'democratize beauty for consumers across segments.' She knows the sweet spot to ride the opportunity that urbanization and upward mobility of Indian consumers offers. Reliance not only has the staying power, but they also know the importance of unit economics. Remember what Reliance did for data with Jio? They completely disrupted mobile telephony by giving access to literally every Indian who could afford an inexpensive smart phone. Even Reliance, with its huge cash reserves doesn't burn cash for as long as VC-funded startups do. They penetrate markets aggressively and quickly raise prices to become profitable or have the economies of scale to make at lower costs than competition for consumer product brands. They also always keep in mind affordability and offer lower value packs to cater to consumers in real Bharath. Reliance retail is also launching an inner wear brand Brush Lace, to create an affordable yet aspirational brand for women.

While we are talking about the Reliance group, RIL just launched the Jio Bharath 4G smartphone at Rs. 999! What will this do? It will help the 250-300 million Indians still on 2G to move up to 4G with a Jio Sim of course and that would most probably be their SIM for life! Talk about creating a platform with a product, for Customer Lifetime Value for their service offering. This is the way to cater to the real Bharath in style. Jio is packaging this with 30% discount on data and 14 GB of data and unlimited Voice at Rs. 123. This is significantly more data than the other Telcom companies give with their feature phones. Reliance is also supposedly creating an entire ecosystem called the Jio Bharath Platform that mobile manufacturers can build on and Karbonn has already started doing this. So, it is like a Play Store that Integrates UPI based JioPay, Jio Cinema and other 4G services. This could be a real moat as Warren Buffet says, for Reliance Jio. We don't know how well they will execute this, but this is an example of how Mukesh Ambani thinks and how intimately he and his team understand and serve consumers at the bottom of the pyramid, the middle class, and the really affluent ones, across industries they operate in.

Now, if you want to succeed as a mass-market brand in India then you should know one thing – Volume is King and Value is a mere shadow of Volume. You cannot build and price for the urban affluent and expect the masses to buy. They sadly still cannot afford it. Will this change? Hell, yes, but it will take another 30 or so years and you must be in business till then to ride that wave. India is making phenomenal strides economically and is the 5th largest economy in the world today. India will go on to becoming the largest economy in the world in the next 30-40 years with its phenomenal demographic dividend. So, companies that are profitable, start small and stay in business for long enough are going to reap tremendous rewards. Those that have to give VCs exits in 7 years will be successful only if they have the correct products, healthy margins and address a pressing urban problem or a problem at scale with great unit economics.

Now do you have to address the entire population of India? The answer is a resounding NO. Do you have to cater to all of India geographically? Again, the answer is NO. Entrepreneurs need to understand who their consumers are and ensure product-market-fit for those consumers. Companies like The Whole Truth Foods are doing a fantastic job of disrupting the unhealthy packaged foods business with very healthy options. They are doing a great job catering to the urban, informed and health-conscious niche. While they too are funded and still loss making, if they scale and price higher over a period of time, they could have a great profitable business. So, while we all talk of the phenomenal opportunity that is India as a whole, it is important to understand that catering to a single state in India is like catering to an entire European country or at times two! I will leave you with a visual capitalist map to let that sink in, so you make sure that you don't spread yourself thin geographically at the start itself.

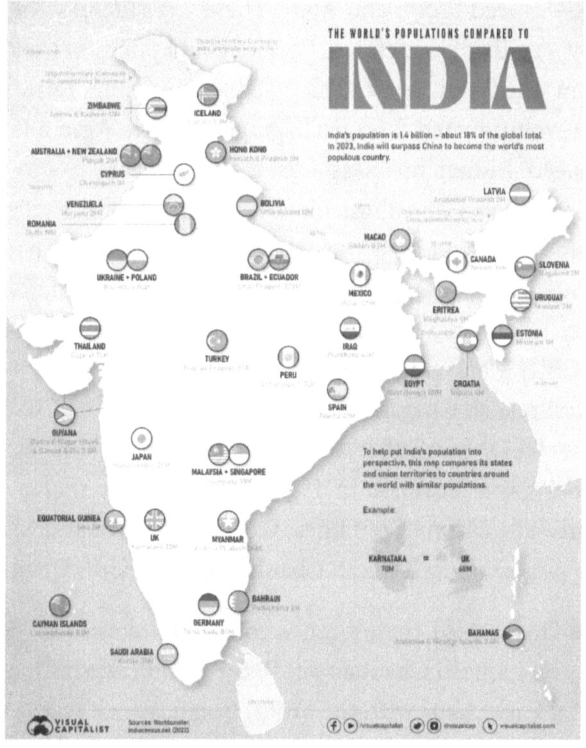

Source: https://www.visualcapitalist.com/population-of-india-compared-with-countries/

* * * * *

Do you Know Frooti? What about Appy?

As a 1980s kid, I, like most others born in the 1980s and 90s loved Frooti and Appy. These were literally the first ready – to-drink fruit juices that we could put in a straw into a tetra pack and drink. The Swedish company Tetra pack had revolutionized food packaging and Parle Agro a family managed Indian business was a first mover in adopting it. It was novel and immediately caught the fancy of most Indians. The company was started by Mohanlal Chauhan in 1929. Mohanlal Chauhan was the great-grandfather of Nadia Chauhan who is now the Joint-Managing Director and Chief Marketing Officer of Parle Agro, controlled by her father Prakash Chauhan. Her older sister Schauna Chauhan is the CEO. Jayantilal, Mohanlal's youngest son, started the beverages business in 1959. The company that owned brands like Thums Up, Limca, Gold Spot, Citra and Maaza, were passed on to Ramesh Chauhan and Prakash Chauhan.

Parle Group sold these brands to Coca-Cola in the 1990s. Post this Ramesh Chauhan got Bisleri and Prakash Chauhan started Parle Agro with the Frooti brand, which was started in 1985, the year Nadia Chauhan was born.

Nadia Chauhan has been groomed by her father since a very young age and apparently used to drop in for meetings at office from the age of 11, after school. Nadia joined the company in 2003 at the age of 17. When Nadia joined the business, she realized the company had a turnover of Rs. 300 crores and 95% of it was from Frooti!

Fast forward to 2023, Nadia Chauhan and her sister have grown the business to a Rs. 8000 crore revenue, profitable, privately held family business, according to BT. Now Frooti contributes only 48% to the top-line. Parle Agro opened several manufacturing facilities across the country and diversified its portfolio, without losing focus on its core beverages business. Nadia launched Appy Fizz which created a new category, between the synthetic carbonated drinks and fruit juices. She changed the white packing which was not working to black, and it was a smashing hit. What was an experimental launch got mass market adoption and created a whole new category of fruit fizzy drinks in India. Appy and Bfizz now contribute 22% to revenues. Bailey the water brand contributes Rs. 1000 crores and more recently Parle Agro has entered the packaged milk products segment with Smoodh. Even here they have got the starting price point of Rs. 10 right for their 100 ml packs of flavoured milk, where most brands had a starting price point of Rs. 15-30 for slightly bigger packs of 150-200 ml. Nadia realized that the penetration of packaged milk is low, and the primary consumers are kids who cannot easily consume more than 100ml. So, Parle Agro seems to have hit the sweet spot and we have to wait and watch to see how this dairy category shapes up as it currently only contributes 6% to turnover.

Nadia refreshed and relaunched Frooti in 2015 and it became a huge hit with its already loyal fan following. So, this case study shows that closely held family businesses can build hugely successful mass market brands and do it profitably.

You should understand that I too have a lot to learn from these entrepreneurs, leaders, brands, and companies and am constantly looking for ways to scale and grow Bril and make it more relevant to today's consumers. This is a journey, and the goal post keeps on shifting. But we must enjoy the journey and cherish the fact that we are still in business and in it with healthy cashflows and profitability, by God's grace.

* * * * *

How Campus Sutra Built a Bootstrapped, Profitable Business

India is so big that there are several segments of the population that a business can cater to and build a profitable business. Campus Sutra is one such company that has done a phenomenal job by serving the aspirational fashion needs of the 18–25-year-old college student demographic. This company was started by siblings Khushboo Agarwal, Aditya Agarwal, and Sonal Agarwal, along with Khushboo's husband Dhiraj Agarwal in 2013. In its first year of business, Campus Sutra clocked a revenue of ₹1.65 crore despite starting mid-year. In the next year it posted a revenue of ₹16 crore, followed by ₹40 crore in the third year of its business. In the fourth year, the company recorded a revenue of more than ₹100 crore. Today the company does close to Rs. 300 crores in revenues with 7-8% ENITDA margins. How is this possible in the ever-changing world of apparels and that too competing against giants like Aditya Birla Fashion and Arvind Fashions? The key to this company's success is its focus on cost management and its understanding of the psyche and aspirational needs of the student population. Campus Sutra primarily caters to students from middle-class homes and does a great job at it. The company sources its products from outsourced OEM factories in India, Bangladesh, and Vietnam. When the Aggarwal's first started, they found a 'haunted' building on

Double Road (CBD) in Bangalore for Rs. 8000 per month and made a 400 sft room their first office. Nobody wanted that building as it was perceived to bring bad luck. When Campus Sutra occupied almost the entire building before shifting out, that tag changed for good. Campus Sutra has cracked the Omni-Channel approach beautifully and today has over 150 employees in locations across India. So, grit, determination, a dogged focus on costs, the right aspirational product and good price-points can do wonders for any business in a populous country like India. The important thing is knowing your consumer and audience intimately and growing with them.

* * * * *

What is Disruption? Is it Good or Bad?

Nowadays every entrepreneur wants to disrupt an industry or something. While this is great and technology specifically has the capability to disrupt or change/ease the way we buy products, services and interact with the world, we must ask ourselves whether what we do is sustainable for the ecosystem. Now, I love technology and it has made life super easy for all of us. Imagine living without Google Maps, UPI (Gpay, Paytm etc), Swiggy, Zomato, Uber and soon AI like ChatGPT! We can't even imagine this right? Having travelled the world, I can confidently say India is right on top when it comes to digital payments. It is indeed an example of positive disruption of old broken systems, that also helps reduce and hopefully completely eliminate black money. The ease of getting registered on a UPI enabled App is so easy that I saw a beggar with a UPI QR code at a signal one day. Yes, no jokes, that is the level of penetration and adoption of digital payments that the Aadhar system and UPI have enabled. Now, when can disruption be bad? I define negative disruption when a company operates below their cost structures to gain market share for prolonged periods of time. Now let me explain this. A company like Uber is a boon, but do you know that it practically wiped out the livelihoods of many small taxi operators in India? Why did this happen? Uber was blowing investor money on huge incentives to drivers and most traditional taxi operators had to shut shop for want of drivers. Now, the drivers invested in 1, 2 or more cars based on the incentives being received. Is this sustainable? No way. Once they had a driver base, Uber started cutting the incentives because they were bleeding like crazy. Now what happens to the drivers? They are in soup. They can't pay their EMIs, and they don't have their old jobs because that company got shuttered for operating at fair prices, above costs. Similarly, Zomato has started reducing delivery partner pay incentives by 40% since 2019. Who gets affected? Again, the poor because the pay and incentives were funded by investor money and unsustainable. The poor delivery boys and girls rely on this income to educate their children and feed their families and do not anticipate a sudden reduction of 40-50%. The bottom line is companies that disrupt in this manner tend to hurt a lot of people including retail investors who have lost a lot of money due to hyped valuations. I very candidly say that this is the kind of business that I do not personally endorse or like. I win, you lose is just not the spirit of intimate leadership. We have to play to build the entire ecosystem in a sustainable manner so all stakeholders benefit. Of course, industries get disrupted and in the normal course of time companies will close down if they do not innovate. But this should happen in the normal course of replacement by other profitable enterprises that can run profitably. Think Kodak, Nokia etc. These companies lost out because of lack of innovation and missing the changing trends in their industries. Personally, managing a small business, even for us changing consumer preferences has not been easy to manage. This is why I owe a lot to luck and the grace of God and take no credit for surviving for so many years. Honestly speaking, though we knew the changing trends and diversified many years ago, we have still faced challenges and headwinds of being associated with Ink only. We keep trying and working really hard by being frugal and delivering great service to our customers and consumers and then hope and pray luck stays on our side to scale further. Though I write about what I do and what my team does, I do not have all the answers and my organization is as vulnerable to changing consumer preferences as any other organization is. As I write this, our cash cow fountain pen inks in Tamil Nadu is being challenged by cheap bigger cartridges from China as children and parents find it less messy and easy to carry. To counter this we are working on various innovations to make carrying and refilling Bril Ink into cartridges easier, including launching a bigger cartridge to create a moat and continue to hopefully dominate the ink ecosystem. While we do everything under our control, it's divine grace that decides the future of market dynamics and whether we exist, survive, or thrive in future.

With the sudden onslaught of AI, tech workers and organizations know how quickly jobs could be lost and organizations could go out of business. Even companies like Google realize the speed at which their moat could vanish and have issued the code red across the organization with the sudden release of Open AI's ChatGPT and Microsoft's $10 Billion investment into it. Google too has released Bard and its reply to ChatGPT. So, I am not against sustainable disruption which is bound to happen. I do not believe in killing small players by operating below costs over a sustained period of time. It just hurts everyone barring the investors and founders who pay themselves or exit at high valuations.

I am very bullish on ONDC, it is a great leveller for D2C and a democratization of access to the digital revolution to the smallest of brands and sellers. It disrupts in a positive way the hegemony and duopoly of Amazon and Flipkart and greatly reduces the costs for small business owners. Also, the access to continuous flow of VC money can never be an answer for a poor business model. The market opportunity of India is huge, and several small entrepreneurs are catering to it beautifully and profitably. Every district in Tamil Nadu for example has multiple homegrown health and hygiene / food / fmcg brands – these are the real heroes. You can be one too!

* * * * *

Get to Know and Mentor Employees' Children

We all want our children to grow up to be successful, peaceful, and happy in life and more importantly be good human beings who care deeply for others. We all want people we respect to take interest and help our children grow. While I don't say all my employees love me and look up to me, I enjoy asking my employees about their children and do my best to make career / general suggestions when they ask me for my opinion. At times, I take the liberty to offer unsolicited advice if I believe in my heart that it would help the child in his/her education/career/life. When any employee wishes for their children to meet me, I happily agree and take on the onus of mentorship. Mentorship is as much for me as it is for my mentee, as it gives me a chance to learn from the next generation.

One example I would like to highlight here is of a boy named Krishna. He is the son of my regional sales manager in Kerala Mr. Balasubramanyam aka Balu. We have a depot in Palakkad, Kerala and Balu and his wife would host me (and continue to host me) for a sumptuous south Indian meal at their home every time I visited Palakkad on work. My visits to their home made me very close to their children Krishna and Karpagam. The mentor in me took over years ago when both these kids were in school. The amazing thing is that both kids were so open to learning and were like sponges. Krishna was always a super smart boy who went on to study MTech in computer science at NIT and was a 10 pointer. After his post graduate studies, he worked with a larger organization before he asked for my advice and joined a startup. He worked with the startup for a few years, but I noticed he was not in a good place. The startup wasn't making revenues and not raising sufficient capital. I was worried he would soon not get paid and worse, his career could suffer if he didn't make a change soon. I felt personally responsible for the career growth and progression of this very smart boy. While I kept warning him, he is genuinely a very nice boy and continued to keep up his promise to the founder. One day he called me and said a fairly big amount was due to him as unpaid remuneration. This was when I put my foot down and told him that he had to startup on his own or join a bigger organization that pays him for his worth and on time. I told him he would stagnate if he continued in this 4-member organization, though he had learnt a lot doing the work and leading tech there. A few months passed and I heard from his father that while he had interviewed with some big brands and got amazing offers, he had still not made the move as the founder of the startup had promised equity a raise and payment of arrears. This is when I took the liberty to call Krishna and tell him to immediately start his own company on the side at least and inform the founder that this is what he wishes to do. I told him that he could work for his employer on project or retainer basis through his new company. After some coaxing Krishna spoke to his boss but his boss wanted him to focus full time as an employee only. This is when Krishna finally called me and said he would startup on his own.

He incorporated a partnership Conscious Technologies to offer high-end software engineering services in AI/ ML, Cloud, iOT, Apps, web development, dashboards, full-spectrum core tech retainer support and more. Upon my advice he also incorporated a Private Limited company to exclusively handle/offer SaaS products he and his team would build along the way to manage their own business. Bril became his first customer as we needed a tech upgradation for our website. He built our new e-commerce website (a progressive web app) ground up and did an amazing job. He has also developed a world-class field-force management and sales app which he will be offering as a SaaS offering to other FMCG and consumer products companies. I introduced him to a few people on my network on pure goodwill basis and they helped him get started and continue to support him. I am delighted and happy to say that his company now has Marquee clients across geographies ranging from USA, Middle East, Asia, and India. He runs a fully remote operation and has a team of 15 people (and rapidly growing) and runs a very profitable business. The great part is that he has built his own project management tools which he will monetize in the months and years to come, to manage his teams. I can say that the tools he has built are as good, if not better than the best SaaS products companies use world-over. Now that his company has growing revenues and profits, I have a commercial arrangement with his company. Today he teaches me so many things and helps my organization in automating various functions and I feel the exhilaration of playing a small part in this person's journey. If you have any tech requirements for your startup/organization, please visit **www.consciotech.com** and call Krishna on **+91-9916784000**. Tell him you read about his journey in my book 😉 I hope and pray children of my employees scale great heights and make their parents, me, and the world proud. Intimate Leadership is way more than transactional employee-employer relationships, it has the potential to form life-long bonds, friendships and hopefully positively impact the next generation too!

* * * * *

That's Not My Job

As a leader it is your duty to set the tone and culture to make people understand that no job is small, and no job is big. Every single person in the organization should be ready to learn and do any task or job for the common mission. When I first joined my business, I could sense huge egos all around. The admin would just not get along with the sales teams. Billing would not happen after 5:30 pm even if money had been received from customers. Stock taking would take priority to servicing customers and this would make sales managers appointed by me mad. Within the despatch department there would be only specific tasks that each person would do, and hierarchy was deeply entrenched. I knew from the very beginning that I had my hands full. Managers had a problem if they had to do packing, so people like Sakthi and Balu would get down and start working with the packers. Once a sample had to be delivered to a customer and the driver was absent. When I asked the manager to deliver it, he said that it was a demeaning task and not worthy of a manager. So, I went to the factory myself, picked up the samples for an important order and hand delivered it myself. In the process I had a good interaction with the customer, and we eventually got that order from the customer who supplied to many schools. Slowly I would push the factory managers to prioritize billing and be outward and sales focussed and shed their unnecessary hierarchical thought process. I would tell them that we have jobs because our customers are paying us. Calls would go to my dad saying they were being asked to stay late and that they are swamped with work. My father was steadfast in his support for me saying the customer should take priority and nobody was asking them to stay beyond working hours every day. As mentioned earlier, this was the period when most of the billing would happen at the end of the month and the last few days required maximum cooperation from every single person in the team. This wasn't happening and egos were so huge that managers would threaten to leave if they had to bill even for an hour after closing time. This happened with multiple managers in our Chennai and Bangalore factories. At one point when a manager in Bangalore said he would leave, I said please do. Not only was he shocked, but the entire team was also shocked. They couldn't believe I had said this. I told people that he wishes to leave, why should I hold him back? I told them that people who wished to stay in this organization had to work for our customers and consumers (We take care of our employees so they can take care of the customers!). How can this be intimate leadership right? While fear is a negative emotion, when employees threaten to jeopardize the organization, it is the time for a leader to say, 'that's it!' We can never allow any individual to hold the organization hostage and jeopardize everyone's hard work. Even though most of the billing and despatch team hardly worked in the first few days of the month, they would refuse to work a few hours extra when the sales teams were toiling in the hot sun and rain to meet targets. The manager quit and I promoted the next in line. The next in line was not very much better but the old ways were too deeply entrenched. Eventually he too quit and we recruited a senior manager from outside. By this time, we had slowly streamlined sales, and billing was happening more evenly through the month with less pressure on the team on the last few days of every month. Despite this new manager coming in and handling the situation much better, the production and admin teams split into the new and the old. Groupism became an issue in our Bangalore factories. I would meet the teams often and tell them that we are all one unit and we had one objective and that is to serve our consumers. I also made it a point to make it clear that we would let go of anyone who would back bite, cause politics or spoil the environment and team spirit. I made it clear that even if the person is a great worker, if he or she had a bad attitude and couldn't get along with people we would be forced to let them go. The mood was sombre initially, but with sales managers like Sakthivel, Balasubramanyam (Balu), our accounts head Padma and my executive assistant Nagendra, we slowly started communicating the customer-first philosophy. We started emphasizing the importance of being intimate and projecting a unified front to the outside world with the ultimate objective of serving our consumers day in and day out. It was not easy because old habits die hard and groupism continued. I do not like using fear in leadership, but sometimes when there are a few rotten eggs, they can spoil the entire basket. So, we let go of a few more people and made our values clear with all new recruits. As the old employees observed this and also started seeing results coming in, slowly but surely, they all started thinking and acting more positively. We also had a reluctant yet very good person at heart, Prabhuswamy, fill the spot of factory manager in a very organic way. So today nobody says it is not my job because we all know that we must wear multiple hats and wear them with pride. Even today when big changes are announced people might murmur a bit, but nobody tries to disrupt the positive energy of the team as they know that it would not be tolerated by anyone in the team. As I mentioned earlier, we are always a work in progress as any organization is, but we are building that army every single day.

I came across this funny yet pertinent story as it happens to varying degrees in most organizations and is in line with the chapter's heading 'That's Not My Job'.

That's Not My Job

This is a story about four people named: **Everybody, Somebody Anybody** and **Nobody**. There was an important job to be done and **Everybody** was sure that **Somebody** would do it. **Anybody** could have done it, but **Nobody** did it. **Somebody** got angry about that because it was **Everybody's** job. **Everybody** thought **Anybody** could do it, but **Nobody** realized that **Everybody** wouldn't do it. It ended up that **Everybody** blamed **Somebody** when **Nobody** did what **Anybody** could have done!

So, as leaders we have to build a culture of **'Hey, let's do it!'**

Have Meetings Outside Office and Team Outings/Offsites in Good Years

While being frugal is important, we at Bril have our sales meetings in good 5-star hotels and at times have a lunch for the teams. Coffee and snacks are a must for all meetings. We change the location and venue each time to encourage group work in different markets so there is organizational exchange of ideas, knowledge transfer and market insights. Moving away from office and meeting in a nice hotel energizes all of us and gets the creative juices flowing. It helps all of us get away from the operational noise and firefighting and focus on the future. It also helps us look forward to a nice lunch occasionally. I make it a point to interact with all the frontline salesmen and understand what is worrying them and what their aspirations are. We not only review the month gone by, but brainstorm ideas for the future. The sales managers make the teams get their monthly, quarterly, and daily target sheets ready and we encourage handwriting SKU-wise targets, so it sticks in the mind. In the age of AI and automation, we must realize that what is in the mind only translates into action. On most years, in April, the sales managers take the teams to some hill-station to brainstorm and plan for the new financial year ahead. I am sharing photos taken after some of these meetings in our factories, hotels and offsites:

Front L-R: Balu (Kerala – AP RSM), Me, Sakthi (TN RSM) with Kerala and TN Sales teams

Me conducting a meeting in Coimbatore.

Team Outing to Kodaikanal

Sales team wearing Bril T-shirts at our Chennai Factory

* * * * *

How do you Identify a consumer problem and positively disrupt an Industry

I always tell aspiring entrepreneurs to look for industries where distribution channels and middlemen have a huge clout. When the internet came it completely disrupted industries like music, books, banking, travel and even consumer products. Now D2C looks at reaching the consumer directly and bypassing the distributor, wholesaler, and retailer. I am thinking more like how can you empower rural women to be your consumer, brand advocate and salesperson. I know HUL's project Shakti has been doing this for years now, but I still feel this is like a side project and they have reached only 160000 rural women so far. I imagine a world where end users are brand ambassadors, salespeople, and micro entrepreneurs. The direct selling businesses like Amway did well till the internet came along, but that involved a lot of recruiting and downlines etc. I am talking about plain and simple purchase and sales transactions at the bottom of the pyramid. At Bril we have started a loyalty program called Bril Members where people who buy online for Rs. 1000 or more are given an opportunity to become a Bril Member and save 15% on MRP on the first purchase and all future purchases; the only condition being they should purchase for Rs. 1000 each time. They get free shipping on all orders. Now, can we have a loyalty program and a bite-sized reseller program for the rural markets? I am sure there is a way if one can crack the logistics hurdles using technology (With smart-phone penetration increasing), connect wholesalers/ retailers to these micro-entrepreneurs and micro-finance their ventures. We have started doing this in a small way in Bril in pockets. Let's see what the future holds......it sure is exciting 😊 Wishing you too the very best in life and in your leadership journey! But wait, before you go, the next and final chapter is super important, so read on....

* * * * *

We Have a Duty towards our Country, as Leaders and as Consumers – Food for Thought

Walk into any supermarket, Kirana shop, retail general store, or wholesale outlet, or visit an online marketplace like Amazon or Flipkart and visit the home care / personal care section. What do you see? You will see brands, right? Of course, you will see consumer products brands. But have you ever asked yourselves whether the brands you see are Indian brands? You will be shocked to note that 70% of the shelf space in the home and personal care categories in most supermarkets and A-Class grocery stores are occupied by Hindustan Unilever brands. 25% shelf-space will be occupied by P&G brands and balance 5% by other brands. In smaller shops and tier-2 and 3 cities and rural markets at least 60% shelf-space will be taken up by HUL, around 20% by P&G and the rest by an assortment of local small brands. I say this based on my visual study over the years in different markets across India (Predominantly South India). HUL has become an integral part of 90% of the households in India, with each of these households using at least 1 product from the HUL stable. HUL has 50+ brands in 15 distinct categories. Many of HULs brands are leaders in their categories and super brands. Why am I talking about this? What is the relevance you ask. HUL of course is as Indian as can be and has been operating in India since the 1930s while P&G has been around since 1950s. I admire and love both these companies and have learnt a lot by studying them over the years, but one thing we need to be clear about is that 61.9% of Hindustan Unilever is owned by UK parent Unilever PLC. 68.73% of Procter & Gamble Hygiene and Health India is owned by P&G USA. "So what?", you say! "HUL and P&G are as Indian as can be and have super brands". You say, "I love their brands"! Of course, and that is exactly the hard-hitting point I wish to make! I like HUL's and P&Gs brands and use them wherever I do not find comparable Indian substitutes, but I am also aware that every time I spend my money on any of these two company's brands, more than 60% of the dividends paid leave India (More than 60% of the market capitalization of these companies are owned by their international parent companies. So, if they do sell their shares, in theory, all the money leaves the country!). More than 60% of the value added by these brands is no-longer technically India's. "So what?" you say, "We live in a globalized world". I totally agree and am not a protectionist, but can you imagine that we as consumers are dependent on foreign brands for our daily-use essential products? Isn't this a shame? If we had to depend on foreign companies for niche / hi-tech segments, it is still fine. Shiv Shivakumar rightly gave an example of NASA in his thoughts on leadership, so I though it is apt to mention that Indian leaders and scientists in ISRO have made India proud by becoming the first nation to land on the south pole of the moon! We are now exploring the sun with Aditya L1, but we are buying soaps, shampoos, and detergents of all things from foreign companies! Isn't it ironic? As Indian leaders and entrepreneurs do we not have to think about why, barring a few amazing companies we have not been able to garner consumer-intimacy and love for products as basic as daily use FMCGs like soaps, shampoos, toothpaste, detergent liquids, detergent powders, floor cleaners and toilet cleaners? Do we not need more super-brands like Parachute Coconut Oil, boldly created and headed by Harsh Mariwala of Marico that take on and beat the HULs of the world at their own game? Marico annihilated HUL's Nihar Coconut oil and eventually acquired it. Parachute is till date a super brand and market leader in its category! As an emerging superpower, India needs many more of its own homegrown super brands in daily-use essential consumer product categories more than ever. Please understand that this book is about all consumer goods across categories, and you would have realized that while reading through the chapters where we covered, FMCG, Apparel, Shoes, Phones, Beverages and more. However, in this last chapter I have made it a point to speak ONLY about the absolute essential FMCG products that we use day in and day out, to make a very important and pertinent point.

We do have many 100% Indian super brands from the following companies in the FMCG space and many of them have market leaders in certain categories, but we definitely need to work together as leaders to make Indian consumers love and choose Indian brands over foreign counterparts. When I posted on LinkedIn about this situation of our dependence on foreign brands for everyday consumption products, people had various opinions and insights. Most consumers felt that:

1. Indian brands lack distribution depth / availability
2. Many of them felt that brand visibility is lacking among Indian brands and
3. Some people said product quality of Indian brands is not at par with foreign brands.

I agree with the first two points but beg to differ when it comes to product quality. Indian brands and Indian OEM manufacturers have as good if not superior quality products to foreign brands in most personal care and health and hygiene home care categories. When India can make and send satellites to space and make rockets land on the moon, making everyday essentials is not 'rocket science' and we do a great job at it. Where we lose out is the ability to tell a moving story to build intimate, enduring brands and top-of-mind recall in the consumers' minds. A lack of consumer-pull automatically reduces shelf space in retail and wholesale, and these amazing products don't get the consumer love they deserve! It's high time we Indian leaders and entrepreneurs crack this branding and marketing code. I for sure am on a mission to do this and hope to get the support from God and my team to execute my Vision for Bril!

I will list a few companies that you as a consumer can consciously choose (like me and my family do), to support top-notch Indian companies and their brands. Buy products from Wipro Consumer Care and Lighting, Marico Limited, Jyothy Labs, Bril (www.brilindia.com), Cholayil MEDIMIX, Vicco Laboratories, Tata Consumer Products, Bajaj Consumer Care, Emami Ltd, Dabur India Limited, Godrej Consumer Products Limited, Himalaya Herbal Healthcare and ITC Ltd to name just a few great FMCG companies with super brands in their respective categories.

Before you read the next paragraph, name/write some of the brands by the above Indian companies. Then name a few brands that are top of your mind. Write them down. Don't cheat.......

Some well-known Indian brands by these companies are Good Knight (Started by Indian Entrepreneur R. Mohan and purchased by Godrej), Parachute Coconut Oil (Marico), Odomos (Dabur), Dabur Chyawanprash (Dabur), Vicco Vajradanti (Vicco Labs), Bajaj Almond Drops (Bajaj Consumer Care), Fiama Di Wills (ITC), Navratna (Emami), Zandu (Emami), Margo (Jyothy Labs), Himalaya (All personal care), Santoor (Wipro), Bril (Stationery and Health and Hygiene products) and in foods we have Amul and Britannia which are awesome brands. But do you notice that we have to think hard and hand pick most of these brands? On the other hand, top of mind we can shout out Surf, Rin, Ariel, Colgate, Pantene, Clinic. Pears, Hamam, Walls, Tresseme, Head and Shoulders, Dove, Pampers, Vicks, Whisper, Harpic and more – All Foreign brands owned by HUL, P&G, Colgate Palmolive, and Reckitt Benckiser!

Since you have read this book, the brands you recalled might have been a bit biased. But I would like you to do another exercise with your mother, father, spouse, children, friends and even grandparents (if you are lucky enough to still have them around). Make the following product list on a blank piece of paper and ask them to name the first brand that comes to their mind beside each product. Don't tell them anything else:

Soap:

Shampoo:

Moisturising Cream:

Toothpaste:

Razor:

Shaving Foam/Cream:

Detergent Powder:

Detergent Liquid:

Toilet Cleaner:

Floor Cleaner:

Dish Wash:

Water:

Diapers:

Analyse your answers and think about who owns majority of the brands listed. I have done this exercise since my B-School days with many people and the results are always 80-90% foreign company owned brands which are top of mind recall for Indian consumers. Unless this changes, we Indian entrepreneurs are not succeeding to our full potential.

So, summing this up – Indian Entrepreneurs have a LOT OF WORK TO DO to get intimate with consumers and build super brands. It takes a lot of work to build distribution depth and get consumer love in a marketplace cluttered with so many brands that are so similar on the emotions they cater to! Having a great product is just not enough if consumers don't know about it – so in FMCG and the consumer products space PRODUCT AVAILABILITY, VISIBILITY AND A RELEVANT EMOTIONAL CONNECT (A good touching story) over long periods of time ARE KEY. Indian consumers must start doing their bit to support Indian companies by buying Indian brands wherever they can. Let us do this as a new-age swadeshi movement so we are self-reliant and don't have to depend on foreign brands for our daily essential consumption.

As I said in the beginning, this book is about Bril and yet not about Bril. So, let me wrap up by urging you to become a Bril Member and buy some world-class stationery and health & hygiene home care products from Bril. Visit www.brilindia.com and become a Bril Member by buying for Rs. 1000 (Get 15% off on MRP on the first and all subsequent Rs. 1000 purchases! Get FREE Shipping Too!).

As a consumer, please do support and spread the word about Bril – a 100% Indian-owned, Made-in-India, Made-For-India, family-managed business, and brand.

Thanks for reading my book and wish you the very best in your Intimate Leadership journey!

Bril® INK AND STATIONERY PRODUCTS
www.brilindia.com
Bril®
Make living fun™

Bril® HOME CARE PRODUCTS
DISH WASH LIQUID
www.brilindia.com
Bril®
Make living fun™

Bril's Home Care range has now been rebranded to B Brilians range of Home Care Products, to give it a unique identity while still leveraging the equity, recall, trust, and love of the iconic, heritage brand Bril:

I would like you to take a very short survey on how you perceive a heritage Indian brand like Bril and how we should leverage its equity in the Home Care Products and other consumer products categories, going forward. Please take a micro-survey and help me out by visiting

https://brilindia.com/bril-and-you

I truly appreciate you taking a few minutes of your time to help me and my team out.

I hope this book added value to your life in some way. Wish you the very best in your 'Intimate Leadership' journey! God bless you!

Reach me at

jayaram@brilindia.com

LinkedIn: https://www.linkedin.com/in/rajaramjayaram/

Other Books by Jayaram Rajaram

Just Invest and Become Insanely Wealthy – Intuitive Investing Across Asset Classes

* * * * *

Appendix

Report Formats you can create on Excel and Use for your consumer-products business.

DSR (Daily Sales Report) to be filled by frontline salesmen:

Salesman Name: City/Town:				
Date: Area:				
Sl. No	Outlet Name	SKU 1	SKU 2	SKU 3
Total				
Total Calls: Productive Calls				

You will need the above if you don't have an automated sales system in place, yet.

Secondary Tracker Sheet or Quarterly Planning Sheet:

PRI – CQLY		SEC TRACKER <Qtr>			
SEC-CQLY		Salesman Name			
Date	CQLY Daily Secondary Sales Average	Current Quarter Daily Secondary Target*	Daily Secondary Achievement	Target Achievement%	Incentive (if target achievement>=100 then 1% X (D-A) else 0
	=SEC CQLY/ Working Days	=CQDS TGT			

Current Qtr SEC TGT		
No Of Working days in quarter		
CQDS TGT	=Current Quarter Sec TGT/No of Working Days in Qtr	
E.g.,		
NO OF DAYS		92
Sunday		13
HOLIDAY		1
MEETING		
Total WORKING DAYS		78

Daily SKU-Wise Target Sheet Filled by Salesmen (Print one sheet for everyday for every salesman):

Salesman Name:	Date:	Market:			Distributor:	
Sl No	SKU Name	Net Retail Price	Monthly Target (Units	Daily Target (Units)	Daily Achievement	Month Cumulative Achievement (Add previous day's achievement to today's achievement)

The above target sheet should come from quarterly planning done distributor-wise, SKUwise for each salesman (three months planned month wise and totalled for the quarter) and then consolidated and reduced to total SKUwise monthly target (Sum of month wise plans for current month across all distributors handled by particular salesman) and SKUwise daily targets (by dividing qtr units target total across distributors for each SKU by days in qtr) for entire territory for each salesman.

Daily Sales Report Consolidation to be sent to CEO/Leadership Team by Managers for All Salesmen (One Salesman per excel sheet):

Date	Tour Program	Area Worked	Total Calls	Productive Calls	Daily Secondary Sales Target *	Secondary Sales Daily Achievement	Secondary Target Achievement%	CMLY Daily Actual Secondary**	Primary Achievement	Daily CTC/Daily Secondary Sales%***

*Figure from Qtr Sec Tracking Sheet

**Take current month last year total secondary achieved by salesman and divide by working days in current month this year

***Calculate salesman's total CTC for the month (Avg TA, DA + Salary) and divide by working days in the month to get Daily CTC. Divide Daily CTC by Daily Secondary Sales Achieved and multiply by 100. This figure should be less than allowable limit for your organization. This should be one of the KPIs.

Total Calls and productive Calls should be an OKR.

SMA or Stockist Movement Analysis (If you have Super Stockists, you will also need a Super Stockist Movement Analysis)

SKU Name	Distributor Price	Opening Stock (Units)	Opening Stock (Value)	Purchases (Primary) Units)	Purchases (Primary Value)	Sales (Secondary Units)	Sales (Secondary COGS Value)	Closing Stock Units	Closing Stock Value

Each distributor will have an SMA. Managers will have to consolidate by adding all distributor Opening Stock (Closing Stock of Previous month will be Opening of current month), Primary Sales and Subtract Bill-wise Secondary sales to get Closing Stock. Consolidated report to be sent monthly to RSM/CEO/ Leadership. This closing stock has to be tallied with actual physical stock taken by salesman for each distributor. If Closing stock is taken few days before month closure, bills raised by distributor after that maybe reduced manually from closing stock to tally figures.

SMPS Primary Sales (daily sales Primary Sales):

Sl. No	SKU	Apr	May	June	Jul	Aug	Sep	Oct	Nov	Dec	Jan	Feb	Mar	Total

Take the Primary units from the SMA for the month and fill into the corresponding month in the above report.

SMPS Secondary Sales (Stockist Movement Secondary Sales):

Sl. No	SKU	Apr	May	June	Jul	Aug	Sep	Oct	Nov	Dec	Jan	Feb	Mar	Total

Take the Secondary units from the SMA for the month and fill into the corresponding month in the above report format.

SRPS (Sales Rep Primary and Secondary):

SR Name	Primary Sales for Month	Secondary Sales for Month
Total		

Please note that the primary sales total of all salesmen should be equal to SMA consolidation primary. However even at distributor rate (i.e., rate that does not factor in distributor margin), secondary value in SMA should always be more than Salesmen's total Secondary in SRPS, unless distributor has sold nothing over and above what the salesman has sold. In such a case salesman's secondary will by SMA secondary total + Distributor Margin (Or retail rate value). This should never happen because the distributor always has to sell on all days while the salesman visits each distributor only for 2-10 days in a month depending on number of distributors he handles.

Quarterly Inventory Planning Format for outsourced manufacturing products (Use with one month as lead time, before each quarter)

Sl. No.	SKU Name	Closing Stock Across Warehouses (A)	Requirement for Current Quarter (Sum total of demand forecast from all areas) (B)	CQLY (Current Quarter Last Year Sales) for reference	Lead Time (1 Month) Demand (C)	Total Additional Orders to Placed (D=B+C-A)	Orders Pending With Suppliers (E)	Fresh Order to be Placed. F= D – E

References

So How Do You Build a Powerful Brand?

https://finance.yahoo.com/news/overview-nike-supply-chain-manufacturing-130048337.html

https://fashinza.com/brands-and-retail/news/who-manufactures-nikes/

https://www.lifewire.com/where-is-the-iphone-made-1999503#

The Golden Ladder Rise to Be Unstoppable by Vijay Parthasarathy

Never Ignore the Power of Feat on The Street

https://en.wikipedia.org/wiki/Ballpoint_pen

Reynolds Pen – History (reynolds-pens.com)

Change of Product, Packaging or Product Design for the Sake of Change Is Disastrous

*https://www.history.com/news/why-coca-cola-new-coke-flopped

So, What Makes Consumers So Passionate About 'Their Coke'? – It's Biochemistry at Work!

'Predictably Irrational' by Dan Ariely

How Indra Nooyi and Shiv Shivakumar Energized PepsiCo

https://www.forbes.com/sites/greatspeculations/2019/12/18/can-coca-cola-bridge-its-revenue-gap-with-pepsico/?sh=698add1c48dc

https://economictimes.indiatimes.com/news/company/corporate-trends/how-chairman-d-shivakumar-is-trying-to-charge-up-pepsico-by-energising-people-who-make-the-brand/articleshow/46615491.cms

https://youtu.be/g_-jS_Dr_a8

https://en.wikipedia.org/wiki/Indra_Nooyi

Think Beyond the Metros and Recruit for Attitude

*https://www.education.gov.in/

* https://indianexpress.com/article/india/more-than-19500-mother-tongues-spoken-in-india-census-5241056/

Pricing and Price Elasticity

* https://www.cnbc.com/2023/04/24/lvmh-becomes-the-first-european-company-surpass-500-billion-in-value.html

https://companiesmarketcap.com/

Investing your Profits in Assets for Future Growth Capital

https://www.propmodo.com/walmart-is-using-its-real-estate-portfolio-to-push-into-e-commerce/

https://seekingalpha.com/article/4050744-wal-mart-sum-of-parts-part-1-reit-worth-current-price-of-stock

India's Bootstrapped Poster Children ZERODHA and ZOHO

https://startuptalky.com/zerodha-trading-services/

https://tradebrains.in/zerodha-success-story/

https://www.moneycontrol.com/news/business/companies/the-zerodha-story-how-the-kamath-brothers-built-indias-largest-retail-broker-3403181.html

https://www.statista.com/statistics/1056530/india-zerodha-number-of-active-customers/

https://economictimes.indiatimes.com/markets/stocks/news/zerodha-may-make-rs-2500-crore-profit-in-fy23-report/articleshow/99059418.cms

https://www.businesstoday.in/entrepreneurship/story/why-zerodha-never-hired-iit-iim-graduates-heres-what-ceo-nithin-kamath-said-367915-2023-01-28

https://yourstory.com/2022/05/the-turning-point-zoho-sridhar-vembu

What I Think About Valuations

https://www.investopedia.com/terms/t/terminalvalue.asp

https://www.youtube.com/watch?v=c20_S-QgvsA&feature=youtu.be

Do Not Be in a Hurry – Patience and Focus Compounds Like Crazy!

https://www.republicworld.com/sports-news/cricket-news/sachin-tendulkar-credits-late-indian-entrepreneur-for-securing-future.html#:~:text=He%20was%20said%20to%20be,crore%20with%20MRF%20in%202001.

*https://www.tyremarket.com/tyremantra/michelin-ranked-valuable-tyre-brand-globally-mrf-apollo-make-top-15/

https://www.nationalheraldindia.com/business/mrf-from-rs-11-on-debut-to-rs-1-lakh

https://www.linkedin.com/posts/saurabhsinghz_india-success-mrf-activity-7074322343623335936-idho/?utm_source=share&utm_medium=member_android

Just Do It – Take That Risk Your Gut Says Will Be a Gamechanger

https://slate.com/culture/2023/04/air-movie-accuracy-michael-jordan-nike-fine.html

Production Planning

https://www.hollywoodreporter.com/lists/air-movie-cast-guide-michael-jordan-nike-deal/marlon-wayans-as-george-raveling/

AIR Movie

Where's the Real Bharath, and How to Serve It?

https://economictimes.indiatimes.com/news/india/salary-rs-25k-per-month-youre-among-indias-top-10-wage-earners/average-salaries/slideshow/91810331.cms

https://indianexpress.com/article/business/if-your-net-worth-is-rs-1-44-cr-youre-among-1-of-wealthiest-report-8615280/

https://indianexpress.com/article/business/if-your-net-worth-is-rs-1-44-cr-youre-among-1-of-wealthiest-report-8615280/

https://www.financialexpress.com/industry/reliance-retail-set-to-face-off-against-nykaa-womens-inner-wear-new-battleground/3150537/

https://telecom.economictimes.indiatimes.com/news/devices/jio-launches-jio-bharat-4g-phone-at-rs-999-to-drive-2g-mukt-bharat/101461407

https://www.visualcapitalist.com/population-of-india-compared-with-countries/

https://www.dnaindia.com/business/report-meet-nadia-chauhan-jayanti-chauhan-s-cousin-who-built-rs-8000-crore-firm-from-dad-s-rs-300-crore-biz-3049314

How CampusSutra Built a Bootstrapped, Profitable Business

https://www.fortuneindia.com/bengaluru-buzz/the-agarwal-instinct/103791

Do you Know Frooti? What about Appy?

https://www.financialexpress.com/lifestyle/who-is-nadia-chauhan-the-woman-behind-frooti-appy-fizz-success-heres-how-shes-aiming-to-turn-parle-agro-into-a-rs-20000-crore-business/3157348/

What is Disruption? Is it Good or Bad?

https://www.moneycontrol.com/news/business/zomato-curbs-income-of-delivery-boys-may-move-to-a-new-payment-structure-4444641.html

We Have a Duty Towards Our Country as Leaders and Consumers

https://www.businesstoday.in/latest/corporate/story/pg-versus-unilever-how-the-two-global-consumer-giants-are-neck-and-neck-in-india-239069-2019-11-13

https://finshiksha.com/hul-company-analysis/

www.ingramcontent.com/pod-product-compliance
Lightning Source LLC
LaVergne TN
LVHW041153150826
845673LV00001B/145

9798891337336